NEW DIRECTIONS FOR EVALUATION
A PUBLICATION OF THE AMERICAN EVALUATION ASSOCIATION

Gary T. Henry, *Georgia State University*
COEDITOR-IN-CHIEF

Jennifer C. Greene, *University of Illinois*
COEDITOR-IN-CHIEF

# How and Why Language Matters in Evaluation

Rodney K. Hopson
*Duquesne University*

EDITOR

Number 86, Summer 2000

JOSSEY-BASS PUBLISHERS
San Francisco

HOW AND WHY LANGUAGE MATTERS IN EVALUATION
Rodney K. Hopson (ed.)
New Directions for Evaluation, no. 86
*Jennifer C. Greene, Gary T. Henry,* Coeditors-in-Chief
Copyright ©2000 Jossey-Bass Inc., Publishers, 350 Sansome Street, San
Francisco, CA 94104.

Microfilm copies of issues and articles are available in 16mm and 35mm,
as well as microfiche in 105mm, through University Microfilms Inc., 300
North Zeeb Road, Ann Arbor, Michigan 48106-1346.

*New Directions for Evaluation* is indexed in Contents Pages in Education,
Higher Education Abstracts, and Sociological Abstracts.

ISSN 1097-6736        ISBN 0-7879-5430-6

NEW DIRECTIONS FOR EVALUATION is part of The Jossey-Bass Education
Series and is published quarterly by Jossey-Bass Inc., Publishers, 350 Sansome Street, San Francisco, California 94104-1342.

SUBSCRIPTIONS cost $65.00 for individuals and $118.00 for institutions,
agencies, and libraries. Prices subject to change.

EDITORIAL CORRESPONDENCE should be addressed to the eCo-editors-in-
Chief, Jennifer C. Greene, Department of Educational Psychology, University of Illinois, 260E Education Building, 1310 South Sixth Street,
Champaign, IL 61820, or Gary T. Henry, School of Policy Studies, Georgia State University, P.O. Box 4039, Atlanta, GA 30302-4039.

www.josseybass.com

Printed in the United States of America on acid-free recycled paper con-
taining 100 percent recovered waste paper, of which at least 20 percent is
postconsumer waste.

# Editorial Policy and Procedures

*New Directions for Evaluation,* a quarterly sourcebook, is an official publication of the American Evaluation Association. The journal publishes empirical, methodological, and theoretical works on all aspects of evaluation. A reflective approach to evaluation is an essential strand to be woven through every volume. The editors encourage volumes that have one of three foci: (1) craft volumes that present approaches, methods, or techniques that can be applied in evaluation practice, such as the use of templates, case studies, or survey research; (2) professional issue volumes that present issues of import for the field of evaluation, such as utilization of evaluation or locus of evaluation capacity; (3) societal issue volumes that draw out the implications of intellectual, social, or cultural developments for the field of evaluation, such as the women's movement, communitarianism, or multiculturalism. A wide range of substantive domains is appropriate for *New Directions for Evaluation;* however, the domains must be of interest to a large audience within the field of evaluation. We encourage a diversity of perspectives and experiences within each volume, as well as creative bridges between evaluation and other sectors of our collective lives.

The editors do not consider or publish unsolicited single manuscripts. Each issue of the journal is devoted to a single topic, with contributions solicited, organized, reviewed, and edited by a guest editor. Issues may take any of several forms, such as a series of related chapters, a debate, or a long article followed by brief critical commentaries. In all cases, the proposals must follow a specific format, which can be obtained from the editor-in-chief. These proposals are sent to members of the editorial board and to relevant substantive experts for peer review. The process may result in acceptance, a recommendation to revise and resubmit, or rejection. However, the editors are committed to working constructively with potential guest editors to help them develop acceptable proposals.

Jennifer C. Greene, Coeditor-in-Chief
Department of Educational Psychology
University of Illinois
260E Education Building
1310 South Sixth Street
Champaign, IL 61820
e-mail:jcgreene@uiuc.edu

Gary T. Henry, Coeditor-in-Chief
School of Policy Studies
Georgia State University
P.O. Box 4039
Atlanta, GA 30302-4039
email: gthenry@gsu.edu

# CONTENTS

# EDITOR'S NOTES

A few months ago, right about the time the contributors for this special issue were preparing their manuscripts, a colleague from New Zealand raised a timely point on EvalTalk, an Internet listserv sponsored by the American Evaluation Association, regarding a then-recent but oft-provoked debate over evaluation terminology and concepts. Commenting on a recent flurry of activity regarding commonly used terms in evaluation (such as input, process, output, outcome, impact, and so on), David Earle came to a conclusion that dovetails nicely with the focus and aim of this special issue: "The thing that strikes me is that evaluation really does have a problem of language. . . . My view is that this all goes to show that evaluation is much more art than science. . . . It also reflects that evaluation is not only interdisciplinary but also very much influenced by our contexts."

Though Earle's comment was stimulating and had the potential of opening another can of worms related to his subject, language in evaluation, EvalTalk was silent as if his comments were either deafening or required more thought from our collegial audience. We heard him loud and clear and had already begun to contemplate the issue before his posting, so we view his comments as a timely opportunity to give attention to the problem and function of language within the evaluation profession.

While attention to language issues is well accepted in social science research, focused consideration in evaluation research and practice is more elusive and limited. The germ for this special volume, in fact, arose out of my attendance at a panel session at the International Evaluation Conference in Vancouver—Evaluation '95. It was there that senior scholars in evaluation, most of whom are featured in this volume, addressed the importance of language in promoting evaluation use and suggested that language was important in developing relationships with diverse stakeholders, particularly in sociocultural settings. As a then-graduate student in sociolinguistics and educational evaluation, my metaphorical light went on: perhaps by understanding the relationship between language and evaluation, significant contributions could be made to the theory, practice, and methods used by evaluators. It had not occurred to me until then that the study of language in its socioeducational context could be extended to an evaluation context.

This volume takes a stab at this relationship. It contributes specifically to a void in the evaluation discipline and generally to emerging interdisciplinary research on the role language plays in interpreting social contexts. Ultimately, this issue is intended to expand and spark new and thoughtful discussion on *why* and *how language matters* in evaluation.

1

## Volume Focus and Aims

The focus of this special issue is to consider and illuminate how language shapes meanings of the social policies and programs we evaluate. The volume offers interdisciplinary perspectives on these language issues, as evidenced by the academic backgrounds and specializations of the contributors. These diverse contributors engage from their various positions and frameworks in discussions of language *of* and *in* evaluation, all designed to advance our thinking in the evaluation community. They purposefully consider how and why language is an evaluation issue and what conceptual or practical concerns and issues are also highlighted by this attention to language. This issue reveals that a number of critical constructs, including race, culture, power, and gender permeate the relationship between language and evaluation. It is therefore important for evaluators to competently understand the role language can play in including or excluding certain stakeholders during the evaluation process. Making sense of language and communication within the often diverse cultural contexts of program beneficiaries, staff, and policymakers further connects issues of language to contemporary discussions on democratization in evaluation.

Distinguishing language *of* and *in* evaluation is a prerequisite for understanding why and how language matters in evaluation. Language *of* evaluation refers to the terms, concepts, and associated meanings that help set the frame for evaluation. In simple terms, it is most often characterized as the language used by evaluators, researchers, and policymakers. Generally technical, it separates the evaluation community from other disciplines and profession-oriented communities, allowing us to speak to ourselves intellectually and conceptually. Language *in* evaluation refers to the language in which evaluation questions, data, and results are cast; therefore it refers to the ideas and values that become privileged in discourse about the social policy or program being evaluated. Evaluating a welfare reform initiative by assessing how many people "get off welfare" is substantively and politically different from evaluating the same initiative by assessing the nature and scope of "meaningful work opportunities" identified by former welfare recipients. Attention to language *in* evaluation points to the importance of stakeholder inclusion in evaluation, of listening to the language of especially diverse program beneficiaries, and to the concepts, experiences, and value stances this language captures.

The challenge, as many contributors in this volume see it, is a return to our colleague's comment on EvalTalk: language needs to be used with great care and attention to the subtleties and nuances of culture, context, and setting. Elizabeth Minnich captured it well in her book when she was framing the need to reconsider the way we think about meanings and expressions of the dominant culture (specifically the representations inherent in higher education curricula) that often exclude and devalue certain types of knowledge and certain types of voices. She wrote that "listening to the voices of others, we also notice the easily forgotten obvious: even when we are all speaking the same languages, there are many other 'languages' at play behind and within what the speakers mean and what we in turn understand." By "becoming aware of the levels and levels of different meanings in even the most apparently simple and accessible utterance," Minnich suggests we could "hear better, comprehend better" (1990). When we are more thoughtful to the issue of language *of* and *in* evaluation, we hear ourselves and beneficiaries better and subsequently conduct better evaluations.

## Volume Layout

The chapters in this volume provide a balance of conceptual analysis and practical advice to the evaluator with frequent use of examples from the field. The volume is organized with this balance in mind. The first set of chapters following the Patton overview focus on how the language of social policies and programs is usually the language of the dominant majority or the powerful elite, and how evaluation and evaluators can work to make this dominant language explicit and to challenge it by incorporating language connoting other concepts and worldviews. The second set of chapters, beginning with the Brown chapter, more specifically address language as part of the evaluation craft and illustrate how careful attention to language can improve what we do.

## Acknowledgment

I am particularly grateful to the editorial and constructive comments of Michael Quinn Patton who helped guide this special issue from inception to final draft. Others have played an important role in helping with patience and clarity during the preparation process. In addition to the contributing authors, they include Craig Russon, Ernie House, Jennifer Greene, and the editorial board of *New Directions for Evaluation*.

Rodney K. Hopson
Editor

## Reference

Minnich, E. *Transforming Knowledge.* Philadelphia: Temple University Press, 1990.

RODNEY K. HOPSON *is an assistant professor of education in the Department of Foundations and Leadership, School of Education, and a faculty member in the Center for Interpretative and Qualitative Research at Duquesne University in Pittsburgh.*

1

*Sensitivity to and skillful use of language are core evalua-tion competencies. The language we use, both among our-selves and with stakeholders, necessarily and inherently shapes perceptions, defines "reality," and affects mutual understanding. Whatever we seek to understand or do, a full analysis will lead us to consider the words and con-cepts that undergird our understandings and actions—because language* matters.

# Overview: Language Matters

*Michael Quinn Patton*

Words are loaded pistols.

—Jean-Paul Sartre

At the very beginning of an evaluation process, I like to bring together the people I'll be working with—program staff, funders, participants, adminis-trators—to lay the groundwork for the evaluation. I usually start by writing the word "*EVALUATION*" on a flip chart and asking those present to freely associate with the word. They typically begin with synonyms or closely related terms: assess, measure, judge, rate, compare. Soon they move to connotations and feelings: waste, crap, cut our funding, downsize, attack, demean, put down, pain, hurt, fear. The word *evaluation* is one of the bullets in Sartre's pistol.

Language matters. This is hardly news, but because language matters so much, it behooves us as a profession to periodically reflect on how and in what ways language matters. This volume is an invitation to such reflec-tion. Such reflections will, I hope, contribute to greater precision, sensitiv-ity, and deliberateness in our use of language.

## Evaluation's Language

We name things to call attention to distinctions we believe to be important. Evaluators have many names for types of evaluation:

- Formative evaluation
- Summative evaluation
- Cost-benefit analysis

- Discrepancy evaluation
- Meta-evaluation
- Utilization-focused evaluation

I once made a list of one hundred names distinguishing different types of evaluation (Patton, 1987). How many names do we need in evaluation? Well, consider this listserv posting by Helmut Sell as a frame of reference:

> My mother tongue, lower Franconian, was until recently believed to be the language with the lowest number of different words, namely about 900. Now, a Bushmen dialect has been described which has only about 600 different words. Too bad! Adenauer, in all his speeches as the German Chancellor, reportedly only used 500 different words. A good English dictionary contains about 240,000 entries. How can people effectively communicate with 600 words at their disposition where others use 240,000 (not counting James Joyce's additions)? [Sell, 1999].

Perhaps the best resource for monitoring the changing size of the language of evaluation is Michael Scriven's Evaluation Thesaurus, which, when he finishes the current revision, will come out in its fifth edition. The first edition (1977) has, unfortunately, been lost through the ravages of time (and a tragic fire) and if anyone has a copy, Scriven or I would appreciate hearing from you. The second edition was 140 pages. The fourth edition (1991b) expanded to 390 pages. The fifth edition, in final preparation as this is written, will have 85,000 more words, a crude but informative measure of language and concept development in evaluation during the final decade of the second millennium. It can be only a crude measure because it is more than a reference work:

> Some may feel that a few entries are too partisan to include in a reference work, but the intent is to provide a reference to evaluation as seen from a particular point of view, and that necessarily means criticism of other views from that point of view. If the partisanship seems to disqualify the book as a reference, one might view it as a very short text (namely, the introductory essay "The Nature of Evaluation," which is 12,500 words) attached to a very long annotated glossary (the rest of the book).

Scriven's disclaimer here, from the draft preface to the fifth edition, is enlightening because, in a sense, it acknowledges that the language of evaluation is rarely, if ever, neutral. Language use inherently depends on point of view. Even supposedly fundamental technical terms such as goals, measurement, validity, reliability, and methods generate debate about their definitions and generality of application. They require context to be clear about their meaning, and that context includes cultural and paradigmatic assumptions. For example, whether people and organizations actually have or act on "goals" (which assumes a kind of linear-sequential, rational mind-set or organizational culture) is a matter of controversy (Patton, 1997, p. 179) and problems with the narrow focus on goals led Scriven (1972) to propose "goal-free evaluation." Whether "validity" is a meaningful term in qualitative research is being debated on a qualitative methods Internet listserv as this is being written. Scriven, who has thought about these matters as much as anyone, has offered a special comment for this volume:

> Nearly sixty terms are equivalent to *evaluation* in one context or another. Begin with a primary list of terms approximately equivalent to the verb *evaluate:* adjudge, appraise, analyze, assess, critique, examine, grade, inspect, judge, rate, rank, review, score, study, test. A longer list, involving nouns as well as verbs and including a number of terms that are used only evaluatively in special contexts would add: accredit(ate), adjudicate, allocate, apportion, appreciation, assay, audit, benchmark, beta-test, check, checkup, classify, comment, consider, criticism, determination, distribution, estimate, finding, field test, follow-up, gauge, interpretation, investigation, mark, measure, monitor, overview, proofing, quality control, perspective, referee, report, "road test" (or "test drive," both now used metaphorically as well as literally), scale, scrutiny, sea trial, survey, synthesis, tryout, valuation, validation, verdict, and weigh.
>
> The rich and subtle language of professional evaluation today is an offspring of the huge natural language resources on this topic and the ever growing metaphorical and technical vocabulary of the discipline, in which terms such as *the jurisprudential model* and *meta-evaluation* are widely used. The language reflects not only the immense importance of the process of evaluation in practical life, but the explosion of a new area of study, long denied that status by the doctrine of value-free science. The language exhibits the whirlpools and eddies of disagreement as well as the tide of a developing core subject and provides a difficult challenge for evaluators to exhibit their eponymous skills in the very process of expressing their own position and conclusions.

## Evaluation Jargon

I once asked Scriven, who has probably identified and named more evaluation concepts than anyone else in the field, how he came up with new terms. He replied that he really didn't like "muddying up the field" with a lot of jargon, so he created a term only when he felt it was absolutely necessary. He said that as he noticed confusion about some issue or became sharply aware of some gap in the field, he would find it necessary to create some new terminology or to offer a new concept to help sort out the confusion and fill in the gap.

I've been known to engage in such efforts myself. I introduced the term "developmental evaluation" (Patton, 1994, 1997) to describe certain long-term, partnering relationships with clients for purposes of ongoing program or organizational development. This naming emerged in designing an evaluation that could not be adequately described as either formative or summative. The developmentally oriented leaders in this program didn't expect (or even want) to reach the state of model "stabilization" required for summative evaluation, and their ongoing funding required no summative decision. Moreover, they attached a special sense to continuously developing their program rather than "just" improving it; nor did they resonate to the connotation that formative evaluation should lead to summative evaluation (Scriven, 1991a). It was helpful in this situation, then, to create a label that had meaning for those involved, so we called it developmental evaluation. Thus does our evaluation language become more specialized. Thus does it also become confusing—and full of jargon.

I encounter considerable frustration about the proliferation of evaluation jargon and confusion about what various terms mean. In the context of this volume, I would share two conclusions I've reached.

First, I don't expect the field to reach agreement on definitive definitions for a great many common terms such as outputs, outcomes, impacts, results, performance—add your own terms of choice. About every three months or so on EvalTalk, the Internet listserv sponsored by the American Evaluation Association, someone posts a request for the "right" definition of some core term, or asks whether evaluation and research are the same or different, or whether performance monitoring is the same as evaluation. A debate flourishes for a few days followed by laments that there is no agreement and wonderment that people can call themselves a profession when they can't even agree on the meaning of a few basic terms.

This evaluation Tower of Babel is a function of the fact that different people and organizations throughout the world use these core words in different ways within their own planning and evaluation frameworks. I see no standardization of language on the horizon. Therefore, it is incumbent on every evaluator to be clear about what she or he means by key terms used in specific contexts, including especially the term "evaluation," and to work with stakeholders to develop shared definitions and meanings for each specific evaluation process.

All the chapters in this volume carry some version of that message, it seems to me. Each author in some way reminds us that we each have a responsibility to be clear about the language we use and understand the implications of our preferred words, definitions, and evaluands for our work and our relationships with those involved with us in our work. In this postmodern age, we will not get definitive universal definitions any more than we will get definitive universal truths. As Jennifer Greene has observed about "practicing evaluation postmodernly," we will have to toil on "and learn to live with its ambiguities and uncertainties" (1998, p. 44).

The second observation I would offer is that jargon is inevitable. It is one of the things that defines professions (House, 1993, p. 25). My teenage son reacted to the jargon he heard me use by starting to express his feelings with nonsense words he made up. To his surprise, those words took on meaning and became part of our family jargon, supporting intimate connection rather than alienation and separation, part of a process I experienced as so transformational that I wrote a book about it to help me make sense of it (Patton, 1999).

Don Miller, who wrote *The Book of Jargon,* says that he began that book with the intent of attacking and making fun of the jargon in various professions. To his surprise, he came to respect it. Whether within families, communities, peer groups, or professional associations, specialized language can add nuance and precision to communications and can support a connection:

> I began to feel that there was something to be learned from the jargons and that in fact it was much more interesting to have these different intellectual dialects in existence than to live in a perfectly homogeneous linguistic universe. . . . It is not only the major professions and subcultures that have their own styles and vocabularies; many smaller social units do, as well. Often within a single family, between brothers and sisters, or between lovers or old friends there exists a special, secret language, unknown to the rest of the world, which carries an intimate set of meanings and associations. In my own experience I have found these to be among the most beautiful forms in which language can be used [1981].

He then decided that the problem was not the existence of jargon but rather its use by those who would exclude, obfuscate, arrogate, or otherwise make themselves unintelligible or superior. He reminds us that "the purpose of language is nothing more or less than communication: and I am proposing, therefore, that language is 'good' only when it communicates, and 'bad' only when it does not" (Miller, 1981).

Jargon, then, is neither inherently good nor bad. Appropriately used, it can deepen communication. To determine its value, we must examine how it is used in a specific context, by whom, to communicate what, with what purposes and effects. The authors in this volume share, it seems to me, both Miller's values about "good" communication and his criterion for evaluating language use. Let me turn, then, to a preview of this volume.

## Social and Political Effects of Language

Anna Madison illustrates the social and political effects of language on program design, policy development, and, therefore, evaluation by looking at the language and labeling of "at-risk youth." She examines the stereotypes and assumptions behind this labeling and the consequences of those stereotypes and assumptions for goal setting and outcomes measurement. She then illustrates the role the evaluator can play in helping stakeholders examine language by facilitating a transition from correcting the deficiencies subsumed in the concept of "at-risk youth" to the goal of "promoting healthy development for youth."

Madison's analysis is a specific example of one of the larger conceptual transformations occurring in policy and program development in many arenas of action, so it may be worth making explicit the larger linguistic context that her chapter illuminates. The idea of "assets analysis" has emerged, in part, as a way of calling attention to a conceptual weakness in the usual way planners and evaluators think about "needs assessment." The idea of assessing client needs is one of the most important in the profession. A number of evaluators, most notably Michael Scriven, have made needs assessment the first and most fundamental step in program development and evaluation. The funding of many programs is contingent on conducting some kind of needs assessment. The concept of needs assessment calls attention to the idea that programs should serve client needs—not staff needs, political needs, organizational needs, funder needs. First and foremost, programs of all kinds should meet client needs.

Needs assessment is a powerful conceptual frame, perhaps too powerful say those who express concern that the focus on client needs has become so pervasive and dominant that program staff and evaluators have largely ignored client strengths and assets. Assets analysis is not the opposite of needs assessment. Rather, it highlights a different aspect of the assessment process. Where needs assessment suggests deficiencies to be corrected, assets analysis calls attention to strengths that can be developed. Just as programs are often unaware of the needs of their clients, so too they are often unaware of the capabilities of their clients. Those strengths or assets, if known, can be used to help clients meet their own needs. Thus we have witnessed great interest in identifying community assets (Kretzmann and McKnight, 1997; Mattessich and Monsey, 1997), organizational assets, and youth assets (Leffert and others, 1998). Assets analysis provides a counterbalance to needs assessment. Both phrases are examples of how the language we use directs our attention toward some things and away from others, a common theme of this volume.

## How Language Frames What We Understand and Do

Rodney Hopson and others examine the language, labeling, and conceptualizations that have affected policy and program development in interventions aimed at treating, controlling, and preventing HIV/AIDS infections at both the individual and community levels. They show how evaluation and outcomes measurement derive directly from the way policymakers and medical practitioners have conceptualized and communicated about HIV/AIDS. They then make a compelling case for including in any policy analysis or program evaluation the perspectives of those living with HIV/AIDS with special attention to the language they use in thinking about what has happened to them and what it means. They also suggest that such sensitivity and understanding can contribute to more effective interventions derived from the experiences and insights of those most affected by HIV/AIDS programs and policies, a conclusion that has relevance to a broad range of programs and policies.

Kenneth Cabatoff examines evaluation language as a tool of policy learning in yet another major arena of action in industrialized societies: the political effort to mobilize support for moving people from welfare to work. Using Quebec province as a case study, he looks at how different advocacy groups frame the problem in ways that affect evaluation criteria and measures. Cabatoff's article reminds us that, in a larger sense, sensitivity and attention to language involve examining the overarching linguistic and conceptual frameworks that ultimately determine the legitimacy of specific evaluation designs and measures. Those frameworks are also the bridge between policy-level analyses and program-level evaluations.

## Sociolinguistic Dynamics

Courtney Brown examines the sociolinguistic dynamics of gender in focus groups. She presents data on how men and women responded to questions in mixed-sex focus groups. She found different patterns of participation depending on the extent to which questions were structured or unstructured. She concludes that the conversational patterns employed by men create an imbalance of participation in focus groups, especially as a result of the "very aggressive" approaches men used to "take the floor," especially by interrupting others. She then examines the implications of "this silencing of women" for the quality and validity of data derived from mixed-gender focus groups for purposes of evaluation. She calls for focus group moderators to pay particular attention to and anticipate the ways in which differential participation patterns can skew evaluation findings.

Beyond her specific findings about focus groups, Brown's article reminds us that sociolinguistic dynamics involve sensitivity to more than just words and concepts. She examines how social interactions, socialized patterns of expression, body language, eye contact, feedback from others, group norms, time available for speaking, differences between structured and unstructured responses, and the role of a group facilitator/moderator, among other factors, affect the data available for evaluative analysis—the actual words in transcripts and the themes that emerge from content analysis of those transcripts. The effects of gender, ethnicity, age, education, and socioeconomic status are manifest through variations in expression, length of response, depth of response, quality of response, and focus in response—all of which affect the ultimate depth and quality of an evaluation.

## Metaphors

Metaphors shared by a group can provide important insights into the constructed meanings of overarching frameworks. Alexis Kaminsky illustrates this point by examining the metaphoric language of evaluation, specifically "the linguistic legacy inherited by evaluation from the social sciences." Kaminsky peels the onion of multilayered evaluation language to expose "deep," "strong," and "emphatic" metaphors.

Kaminsky joins a long line of distinguished evaluation observers who have suggested that evaluators can improve their communications with a variety of stakeholders by using metaphors more consciously, explicitly, intentionally, and emphatically. Bill Gephart, in his 1980 Evaluation Network presidential address, drew an analogy between his work as a watercolor artist and his work as an evaluator. Gephart compared the artist's efforts to "compel the eye" to the evaluator's efforts to "compel the mind." Both artist and evaluator attempt to focus the attention of an audience by highlighting some things and keeping other things in the background. He also examined the ways in which the values of an audience (of art critics or program decision makers) affect what they see in a finished piece of work. Nick Smith directed a research on evaluation program in which he and others thought about evaluators as poets, architects, photographers, philosophers, operations analysts, and artists (Smith, 1981). They consciously and creatively used metaphors and analogies to understand and elaborate the many functions of program evaluation.

Those inclined to include some playful creativity in their interactions with stakeholders may want to consider an approach used by Oswick and Montgomery (1999). They developed metaphoric interview questions to capture internalized organizational images that, they believe, can affect performance and effectiveness. For example, they asked: If you were to compare your organization (or program) to an animal, what animal would it be? They interpreted images of heavy and slow-moving animals as exemplifying low levels of change activity while lean and fast-moving animals suggested an adaptive organization responding to a turbulent environment. They interpreted their findings to illustrate the utility of metaphor in the study of organizations. Their findings might be applied creatively to introduce some fun into a participatory evaluation process, but I wouldn't be inclined to make too much of the results.

Metaphors can open up new understandings and enhance communications. They can also distort and offend. At the 1979 meeting of the Midwest Sociological Society, a distinguished sociologist, Morris Janowitz, was asked to participate in a panel on "the cutting edge of sociology." Janowitz took offense at the "cutting edge" metaphor:

> World War I and World War II, Korea and Vietnam have militarized our language. "Cutting edge" is a military term. I am put off by the very term cutting edge. Cutting edge, like the parallel term breakthrough, are slogans which intellectuals have inherited from the managers of violence. Even if they apply to the physical sciences, I do not believe that they apply to the social sciences, especially sociology, which grows by gradual accretion [Janowitz, 1979, p. 601].

A common theme in this volume is the need for sensitivity in the use of language, with special attention paid to the meanings of words used by program participants and other stakeholders. As the Janowitz example reminds us, language that appears quite unobjectionable to one person can be viewed by another as quite offensive. Evaluators must be particularly sensitive in their selection of metaphors to avoid those with possible racist and sexist connotations, such as "It's black and white." At a conference on educational evaluation and public policy sponsored by the Far West Regional Laboratory for Educational Research and Development, the Women's Caucus expressed concern about the analogies used in evaluation—and went on to suggest some alternatives:

> To deal with diversity is to look for new metaphors. We need no new weapons of assessment—the violence has already been done! How about brooms to sweep away the cobwebs of our male and female stereotypes? The tests and assessment techniques we frequently use are full of them. How about knives, forks, and spoons to sample the feast of human diversity in all its richness and color? Where are the techniques that assess the deliciousness of response variety, independence of thought, originality, uniqueness? (And lest you think those are female metaphors, let me do away with that myth—at our house everybody sweeps and everybody eats!) To deal with diversity is to look for new metaphors [Hurty, 1976].

Metaphors and analogies can be overused. If an analogy is too obtuse or if the point is stretched too far, it loses its power. Properly used, however, metaphors and analogies can facilitate communication, supplant obscure jargon, and illuminate findings. As Thoreau said, "All perception of truth is the detection of an analogy."

## Language, Evaluator Roles, and Evaluation Purposes

Another arena of controversy concerns appropriate roles for evaluators in relation to different purposes of evaluation. Sharon Rallis and Gretchen Rossman examine the evaluator as "critical friend" when the primary purpose of evaluation is learning. In order to play the role of critical friend, they argue, evaluators need to learn how to engage in "dialogue" instead of relying upon the traditional evaluator's "language of authority." They present contrasting examples of evaluation reports to illustrate the distinctions they make. More generally, their work illustrates the close connections between evaluator roles, evaluation purposes, reporting styles, and language.

## Languaculture: A Conceptual and Analytical Framework

Michael Agar offers evaluators an opportunity to learn how organizational development consultants use the study of "languaculture" to understand how people in an organization or community make sense of their world. He uses an ethnographic evaluation of a tuberculosis screening program in Baltimore to show the analytical power of identifying and interpreting "linguistic rich points" and "border lessons." He uses language as a source for concept-based analysis, model building, and relational analysis. Within the overarching organizational development framework he used, he concludes that "attending to language as a surface representation of what programs are all about certainly proved useful" for evaluation.

Other organizational development analysts echo his conclusions about the importance of language for understanding program contexts and dynamics. Ford (1999) used "conversationally constructed realities" to analyze how staff produce and manage change. This framework views conversations as both the medium and product of reality construction within which change is a process of shifting conversations within a communications network. Change, then, entails bringing new conversations into a sustained existence, and the job of change managers is to create the conversational realities that produce effective action. The job of evaluators in such a framework is to document and assess those changed conversations and their consequences.

## Language as Perception-Shaping

> If names are not correct, language will not be in accordance with the truth of things.
> —Confucius

Agar's chapter in this volume on languaculture leads him, in the conclusion, to search for and offer "a new angle of vision on America's enduring issue of race." His reflections on racial divisions remind us of the dilemmas and tensions created in society, and therefore in evaluation, by the categorical distinctions we have inherited. Precipitated by the 2000 constitutionally mandated population census in the United States, the general public has been exposed to the problems and politics of traditional race/ethnicity categories, matters usually debated only by methodologists. We are likely to hear a great deal more debate about the relative merits of a new multiracial census category or of allowing people to place themselves in multiple categories.

In the closing days of 1999, the participants on the Internet listserv EvalTalk had a lively debate about whether an "Other" category should be routinely offered along with the traditional "male" and "female" options to capture more accurately a variety of transgender and mixed-gender people. Another categorical challenge concerns what age groupings to use (and how to label them, for example, "seniors") as populations around the world age.

The language we use to categorize people by gender, ethnicity, age, education, disability, and class, to name but the most common, will affect in fundamental ways how we and others view the people who participate in the programs we evaluate. In his keynote address at the 1998 national conference of the American Evaluation Association (AEA) in Chicago, Professor John Stanfield reminded us that race-based analyses give the impression that racial distinctions have a scientific rather than just political and social basis (Stanfield, 1998). Ten years earlier, at the AEA meeting in New Orleans, Professor Asa G. Hilliard III spoke about how "the images that most of the world now holds about Africa and its people in precolonial and preslavery times are grossly distorted, incomplete, and highly defamatory" (Hilliard, 1989, p. 10). He invited deconstruction of those images and their underlying assumptions to examine how evaluative judgments are influenced by stereotypes embedded in language, thereby maintaining white privilege and power, for "power is the ability to define reality and to get others to respond to that definition as if it were their own" (p. 8). Language, then, is an expression and manifestation of power.

The evaluation language we choose and use, consciously or unconsciously, necessarily and inherently shapes perceptions, defines "reality," and affects mutual understanding. Whatever issues in evaluation we seek to understand—types of evaluation, methods, relationships with stakeholders, power, use—a full analysis will lead us to consider the words and concepts that undergird our understandings and actions, because language matters.

## References

Ford, J. "Organizational Change as Shifting Conversations." *Journal of Organizational Change Management*, 1999, *12* (6), 480–500.

Greene, J. "Balancing Philosophy and Practicality in Qualitative Research." Proceedings of the Stake Symposium on Educational Evaluation. University of Illinois, Champaign, May, 1998.

Hilliard III, A. G. "Kemetic (Egyptian) Historical Revision: Implications for Cross-Cultural Evaluation and Research in Education." *Evaluation Practice*, 1989, *10* (2), 7–23.

House, E. *Professional Evaluation: Social Impact and Political Consequences.* Thousand Oaks, Calif.: Sage, 1993.

Hurty, K. *Report by Women's Caucus. Proceedings: Educational Evaluation and Public Policy Conference.* San Francisco: Far West Laboratory for Educational Research, 1976.

Janowitz, M. "Where Is the Cutting Edge of Sociology?" *Sociological Quarterly*, 1979, *20*, 591–593.

Kretzmann, J., and McKnight, J. *Building Communities from the Inside Out: A Path Toward Finding and Mobilizing Community Assets.* Chicago: ACTA, 1997.

Leffert, N., and others. "Developmental Assets: Measurement and Prediction of Risk Among Adolescents." *Applied Developmental Science*, 1998, *2* (4), 209–230.

Mattessich, P., and Monsey, B. *Community Building: What Makes It Work: A Review of Factors Influencing Successful Community Building.* St. Paul, Minn.: Wilder Foundation, 1997.

Miller, D. *The Book of Jargon.* New York: Macmillan, 1981.

Oswick, C., and Montgomery, J. "Images of an Organization: The Use of Metaphor in a Multinational Company." *Journal of Organizational Change Management*, 1999, *12* (6), 501–523.

Patton, M. Q. *Creative Evaluation.* (2nd ed.) Thousand Oaks, Calif.: Sage, 1987.

Patton, M. Q. "Developmental Evaluation." *Evaluation Practice,* 1994, *15* (3), 311–320.
Patton, M. Q. "A World Larger Than Formative and Summative." *Evaluation Practice,* 1996, *17* (2), 131–144.
Patton, M. Q. *Utilization-Focused Evaluation: The New Century Text.* (3rd ed.) Thousand Oaks, Calif.: Sage, 1997.
Patton, M. Q. *Grand Canyon Celebration: A Father-Son Journey of Discovery.* Amherst, N.Y.: Prometheus Books, 1999.
Scriven, M. "Pros and Cons About Goal-Free Evaluation." *Evaluation Comment: The Journal of Educational Evaluation.* University of California, Los Angeles: Center for the Study of Evaluation, 1972.
Scriven, M. *Evaluation Thesaurus.* (1st ed.) San Francisco: EdgePress, 1977.
Scriven, M. "Beyond Formative and Summative Evaluation." In M. W. McLaughlin and D. C. Phillips (eds.), *Evaluation and Education: At Quarter Century. 90th Yearbook of the National Society for the Study of Education.* Chicago: University of Chicago Press, 1991a.
Scriven, M. *Evaluation Thesaurus.* (4th ed.) Thousand Oaks, Calif.: Sage, 1991b.
Sell, H. "Language." qualrs-l@listserv.uga.edu. December, 1999.
Smith, N. *Metaphors for Evaluation: Sources of New Methods.* Thousand Oaks, Calif.: Sage, 1981.
Stanfield, J. H. "Slipping Through the Front Door: Relevant Social Sciences in the People of Color Century." Keynote speech at the American Evaluation Association national conference, Chicago, Nov. 1998.

MICHAEL QUINN PATTON *is former president of the American Evaluation Association. He received the Alva and Gunner Myrdal Award from the Evaluation Research Society for "outstanding contributions to evaluation use and practice" and the Paul F. Lazarsfeld Award for lifetime contributions to evaluation theory from the American Evaluation Association. He is on the graduate faculty of The Union Institute in Ohio, which specializes in individually designed, nonresidential, nontraditional, and interdisciplinary doctoral programs.*

**2**

*This chapter explores the sociopolitical nature of lan-
guage in evaluation and illustrates the role evaluators can
play as the translator and interpreter in assessing the outcomes of social programs.*

# Language in Defining Social Problems and in Evaluating Social Programs

*Anna Marie Madison*

In evaluation, language serves the instrumental function of communicating
the value or worth of social programs. The language used in evaluating
social programs encompasses the language of social policy, which is interpreted into the technical language of evaluation, which is then translated
into language to meet the informational needs of multiple audiences. Thus,
evaluation is a social process of intergroup communication, a political
process through which conflicts in multiple meanings are resolved, and a
technical process. In this chapter the concept of at-risk youth is used to
illustrate the evaluator's role as an interpreter and translator of the language
used in defining social problems and in developing and evaluating social
programs.

## Applied Linguistics

The field of applied linguistics provides a conceptual framework for understanding the instrumental functions of language in society. Unlike theoretical linguistics, which concentrates on theories about how language is
constructed, applied linguistics concentrates on understanding the social
application of language (Edwards, 1985; St. Clair and Giles, 1980). The goal
of applied linguistics is to contribute to the solution of problems arising in
the use of language in human societies (Bugarski, 1989). During the last
thirty years a considerable body of work has been conducted in the field of
applied linguistics. This work addresses the relationship between language
and society (Edwards, 1985; Halliday, 1978; Lele and Singh, 1989; Tomic
and Shuy, 1989), the sociocultural context of language (Bonvillain, 1993;

Guy, 1988; Halliday and Hasan, 1978; Newmeyer, 1988), the political aspects of language (Pennycook, 1994; Shapiro, 1981; St. Clair, 1980; St. Clair and Giles, 1980), and social identity and language (Edwards, 1985; Gumperz, 1982; Gumperz and Gumperz, 1982).

## Sociopolitics of Language

Ferdinand de Saussure distinguishes between speech as an individual phenomenon and language as social in nature. Language according to de Saussure belongs to the communal storehouse of knowledge (St. Clair and Giles, 1980). The concept of language as a homogeneous collective consciousness assumes that language is unified and constant and gives rise to the concept of linguistic competence (St. Clair and Giles, 1980). Linguistic competence refers to specific standards shared by users of the language that must be adhered to for one to be considered competent in the language. In evaluation this is illustrated by our adoption of communal terms such as *formative* and *summative*, or our common reverences to logical models. Sociolinguists and psycholinguists have challenged the concept of linguistically homogeneous communities as invalid in a society comprised of people who share a common language but who speak variations of that language (Gumperz, 1982; Halliday, 1978; St. Clair, 1980). In evaluation, disputes about labels such as "empowerment evaluation" or about the relevance of "validity" as a criterion in qualitative designs arise from subcommunities within the larger profession. The variety of disciplines involved in evaluation practice is one source of the development of subcommunities.

Shadish, Cook, and Leviton (1991) point out that various communities in evaluation differ in the way they construct reality, and this contributes to differences in the definition of evaluation, the methods of observation, requirements for validations of reality, reporting formats, and evaluation usage strategies. As language becomes more variable, there are likely to be conflicts in meanings. This is especially true as evaluation has become an international and cross-cultural phenomenon. Basic words such as *goals, outcomes, performance measurement,* and *accountability,* to name a few examples, mean widely different things among differing evaluation groups. Anyone reading the Internet listserv EvalTalk or GovtEval knows that these differing definitions can and do lead to conflict.

Sociolinguists note that language becomes sociopolitical when there is intergroup conflict regarding use (Halliday, 1978; St. Clair, 1980). When conflict arises concerning language use, formal language policy provides the standard meaning. Yet, within intergroup communication networks, the contextual meanings are determined by the group. When social groups differ in the meaning of terms, the values of the more powerful group will prevail. The more powerful group will exercise control over the use of language by imposing its standard on the less powerful groups. The sociopolitical context explains the effect of the social structure of language and the exercise of power and control in language use. The history of the debate between advocates of quantitative/experimental/positivist versus qualitative/naturalistic/constructivist paradigms illustrates these changing power dynamics. Some of this debate has centered on such basic notions as whether "truth" or "reality" are meaningful constructs for evaluators.

Using the United States as an example, St. Clair explains that the ideologies of the dominant intellectual, social, political, and economic elite have influenced the development of language and its use as a social tool. He contends that this is done through labeling others as deviant and intellectually inferior, legitimizing the knowledge of those in power, and establishing barriers to social mobility through language and other in-group criteria. St. Clair also points out that labeling is a sociopolitical process used by those in power to establish themselves as the norm (St. Clair, 1980, p. 28). A recent example of this is efforts by some distinguished founders of the field to label "empowerment evaluation" as unethical and deviant (Stufflebeam, 1994).

St. Clair's framework is useful to explain the labeling process as it relates to social problem definitions, social policy, and the evaluation of program outcomes. When viewed from this context, the language of social policy is typically the language of the dominant groups, and it is legitimized by formal bureaucracies. The evaluator may consciously or unconsciously become a social enforcer. The evaluator may choose to prevent the use of labels by introducing alternative concepts, or by creating new meanings in defining concepts. As members of the educated elite, evaluators have the power to make a difference. Thus, in every evaluation, evaluators are faced with the issues of how to label and communicate what is occurring. Differences in purpose labels, accountability, summative judgment, program improvement, knowledge generation, or empowerment will associate the evaluation with certain stakeholder groups more than others.

## The Language of "At-Risk Youth" as a Social Problem and Policy Area

Social scientists (Feldman and Elliott, 1990) report that the absence of adult guidance during adolescence is one the most critical problems facing American society today. There are several factors that contribute to this problem. Change in the American family structure is ranked among the major contributing factors. According to the Carnegie Council on Adolescent Development (1995), over 85 percent of young people ages ten to eighteen will live in a single-parent household at some point. With the single parent working long hours outside the home and the erosion of kinship and community support systems, youth are left on their own. Even in two-parent homes, with the growth of two-worker families, adolescents are spending much of their time with their peers in environments segregated from adults.

Studies of how youth use their unsupervised time indicate that young people who are left on their own, or only with peers, stand a significantly greater chance of becoming involved in substance abuse, sexual activity, and crime than their peers who are engaged in activities under adult supervision (Carnegie, 1992, 1995). From these studies, social scientists conclude that the lack of adult supervision places youth at significant risk of engaging in undesirable behaviors.

Social scientists note that the lack of adult supervision cuts across racial, ethnic, and socioeconomic groups (Dryfoos, 1990). Based upon this interpretation, many youth today from diverse backgrounds are considered to be at risk. However, studies of at-risk youth report that youth from economically disadvantaged backgrounds are often at higher risk than their more privileged counterparts (Carnegie, 1995, p. 47). Sociologists report that young people trapped in ghetto poverty face the hardships of material deprivation, which gives them little hope of a promising future (Schorr and Schorr, 1989). These youth are described as growing up in violent surroundings. Instead of security and protection provided by a supportive and caring family, school, and community, these youth face physical violence, economic insecurity, and uncertainty (Jessor, 1993; Werner and Smith, 1992). Instead of being intellectually challenged in school, their teachers have low expectations of them. Adult role models in their communities are described as more likely to be jobless or working in low-paying jobs. These role models do not raise youth's expectations about jobs and family life (Carnegie, 1992).

The consequences of adolescent neglect reached a crisis proportion during the 1980s. Inconceivably high rates of youth violence, teen pregnancies, adolescent suicides, and drug use among youth startled the nation. Social scientists, politicians, and the citizenry became concerned about the problem. Out of this concern, social program funding was provided by state, local, and federal governments; private corporations; and foundations to combat the problem. The policy language described the target population as "at-risk youth." Thus, the term *at-risk youth* was coined to interchangeably describe both the problem and the youth. Some use the term primarily to describe a category of young people who are a problem to society. This language not only provides social group identity to this category of youth, but the contextual meaning of the language stigmatizes the youth as undesirable rather than the social situation responsible for placing them at risk.

## Evaluation of a Statewide At-Risk Youth Program

The complexities and consequences of the "at-risk youth" language are revealed in the evaluation of a state-level at-risk youth initiative.

**Constructing At-Risk.** In 1994 a state agency commissioned an impact evaluation of its at-risk youth program. One of the first steps was to meet with staff to determine how they defined at-risk youth. They were asked three questions:

- What do you mean by at-risk?
- How will I know an at-risk youth from a youth who is not at-risk?
- What are the indicators of success for your program?

It was interesting to discover that the grantor agency program officer and staff did not have a working definition of what at-risk meant. They assumed that it meant that the young people participating in the funded programs had social problems and the service providers could reduce the magnitude of these problems. They had not clearly formulated initiative goals.

Youth who were not at risk, as distinguished from at-risk youth, were described as youth who are doing well in school, are not getting into trouble with legal authorities, are not involved in substance abuse, and are not teen parents. The youth served by the agencies the grantor was currently funding had the reverse of these characteristics. None of the state staff had any idea as to what an indicator of success for the at-risk youth initiative should be.

When the grantee agencies were asked the same three questions as the grantor, the five most frequent responses for the meaning of *at-risk youth* were:

"An at-risk youth is a low-income kid whose parents don't give a damn about them."

"At-risk youth are kids who are poor and their parents are substance abusers and can't take care of themselves let alone their children."

"At-risk youth are not like my kids or your kids. They come from single-parent homes, their parents are illiterate, and many of the parents are immigrants."

"At-risk youth are minority African-American and Latino kids."

"At-risk youth are youth that everyone else has given up on because of antisocial behavior."

Only one grantee agency out of twenty-eight rejected the label and used the label only to acquire funding.

In response to the question about the differences between at-risk youth and youth not at risk, most of the grantees considered class to be the major stratifying characteristic. As with the definition of at-risk youth, socioeconomic class became the identifier for at-risk. When asked to describe the indicators of success for the intervention strategy, most of the persons interviewed attempted to describe the activities the grantee sponsored rather than the intended outcomes of the programs. Others listed ridiculously unrealistic outcomes such as the reduction of teen parenting by 50 percent in communities having the highest teen pregnancy rates in the state, or the reduction of teen crime by 75 percent in the communities having the highest juvenile crime rates in the state. Three of the agencies wanted to increase the youth's self-esteem and to help the youth to develop coping skills. None of these agencies was confident as to how they would know when this was achieved. Another interesting observation was that the grantee agencies serving all-white youth

chose not to use the term at-risk youth to describe the young people participating in their programs. Yet, their program participants had the same socioeconomic characteristics as the inner-city racial/ethnic minority youth. In
contrast, grantees serving racial and ethnic minority groups felt comfortable
using this term. To these agencies, at-risk meant low-income minorities. In
follow-up interviews with staff in other youth programs, this phenomenon
seems to be widespread. Agencies tend to not use this term when the youth
are white, middle-class suburbanites. The most frequent justification is that
these youngsters (white middle-class) are not at risk because they have two
parents at home or their parents are not poor.

After lengthy discussions with the grantor and the grantee agencies, it
became clear that *at-risk youth* was a label attached to low-income African-
American, Latino, and Asian youth. In this context, *at-risk youth* was a
stereotypical, sociopolitical label. The adjective at-risk was used to describe
a particular kind of youth and to sort youth by ethnic and class social group
identity. Thus, the term at-risk as used in this context places emphasis on
the youth as a category, rather than the risk factors. The language of at-risk
is used as an instrument in the construction of social reality based on the
social values of policymakers, the grantor, and the grantee agencies.

**Consequences of At-Risk Construction.** To the social scientists, at-
risk refers to youth who are growing up without adults guiding and nurturing them in their passage through the critical adolescent developmental
stage. The logic of the social scientist's construction of social reality is that
the absence of adult supervision to guide youth through the tumultuous
period of adolescence leads to youth engaging in undesirable behavior.
Some of the consequences of undesirable behaviors, such as drug use and
early sexual activity, are teen pregnancy and court involvement. This construction of social reality provides a logical link between the risk factors and
the consequences. The social solution is to provide youth-organized, productive, after-school activities that foster healthy psychosocial youth development as a prevention strategy.

The grantor defined at-risk as youth involved in gangs, teen parents,
youth in alternative education, and youth involved in the courts. This construction of social reality is that a particular group of youth places society
at risk. These youth are identified by their circumstances, which are viewed
as resulting from deviant behavior. The logic is that the current condition
is the result of poor choices made by youth that jeopardize their ability to
reach adulthood prepared for productive participation in society. In this construction, the risk factor is the individual and the consequences are lifelong
dependency on society. So the focus of the intervention is on remediation
rather than prevention.

Thus, the grantor agency's strategy is to provide funding to social service providers to help these youth cope with the challenges created by early
parenting or gang involvement. The assumption is that these youth's chances
of fully participating in society as contributing adults can be increased by

engaging them in constructive social activities. This oversimplification of the problem leads to unrealistic expectations about the efficacy of the intervention. The more complicated psychosocial, social, and economic issues are not addressed in the intervention.

The grantee agencies define at-risk youth as low-income, inner-city racial/ethnic minority youth. The social construction of social reality is that the youth are the victims of low-income, uncaring, dysfunctional parents. None of the agencies identified systemic problems, such as educational inequities and structural unemployment, that create economic deprivation and hopelessness as factors contributing to many of the parents' inability to be available to their children. Although the parents are viewed as the risk factor, the future consequences are not clear, nor are the intervention strategies designed to address the risk factor. The logical link between risk and consequences is not provided in the grantees' construction of social reality.

Thus, the grantee intervention strategy was to compensate for the parents because the parents were viewed as the problem. The evaluation revealed that the parents were invited to participate as partners with the agency in only two of the twenty-eight programs. Yet, the Carnegie study (1995) revealed that successful youth programs involve parents as partners. Even if parents participate in only one activity per year, the involvement is valuable to the youth's development. Besides not involving the parents overall, the intervention strategies were unclear, and the intended outcomes were unknown or very unrealistic.

Similarly, the policymakers who sponsored the statewide program viewed at-risk youth as economically disadvantaged youth. This sociopolitical definition places the responsibility for the problem with the parents of these youth. Policymakers, too, fail to address the structural socioeconomic conditions that cause the problem. Instead, the policy language implied that parental neglect was symptomatic of low-income families. By limiting the definition of at-risk to low-income minorities, the developmental problems of middle-class youth are overlooked in the policymaker's construction of social reality. The recent incidents of middle-class youth committing violence against their classmates have made policymakers take notice that middle-class youth are also vulnerable.

In the process of defining at-risk youth, the potential effect on the self-identity of youth is neglected. For the youth, the language of at-risk conjures up personal feelings of anxiety and shame. This shame is internalized by some of these youngsters. In interviews with youth, the term at-risk meant that they are different from other youth. It was apparent that these youth did not like to be identified as at-risk. For some youth, at-risk meant that they are defective in some way. To others it meant that they were "not as good as other youth." Others stated that "people think we are losers and have little potential in life." The youth are aware that at-risk means low-income minorities. Their responses indicate that the label is already having a deleterious effect on their self-image and group identity.

Edwards (1985) notes that when social identities such as class are imposed on a group, they also connote worth. The negative image of lower socioeconomic class labels the individual as being less than others. This may explain why in more than thirty years of conducting social science research and evaluation of programs for the poor, I have observed that not one participant in such programs identifies himself or herself as lower-class. When asked to identify their class, most Americans will describe themselves as working class, lower middle- or middle-class. People are more likely to identify themselves as low-income than lower-class. Whereas both indicate negative worth, the two terms have distinctively different meanings among the poor.

The initial evaluation findings were that the language of at-risk varies. Based on the differences in group values, at-risk meant different things to different people and social groups. Each group assigned a normative value in defining at-risk. Variations in assigned meanings resulted in muddled intergroup communications, as the contextual meaning is interpreted by social scientists, policymakers, the grantor agency (state bureaucracy), and grantee agencies (social service providers) and the youth. The social science research is clear. The language clearly identifies cause and effect relationships. Yet, when the problem is translated into social policy, the policy objectives are unclear. Labels are used to identify the target population. The causal conditions that social policy is intended to address are not identified. In this particular case, the policymakers and grantee agencies tended to use blaming language to identify the parent as the shameful agents. The grantor was less blaming but oversimplified the problem. As each group focused on its construction of the social reality of at-risk, attention to developing successful programming was lost.

**Changing the Language and Reconstructing the Social Reality.** The major problem was that labeling did not allow the agencies to design programs that could have an impact on the social problem. As Baizerman and Compton (1992) observe, to use the concept of risk scientifically, there must be empirical research showing relationships among factors. Since the agencies could not logically link what they perceived to be risk factors to future consequences, it was not surprising that they could not identify those aspects of their programs that would reduce the youth's susceptibility to risk. Therefore, in order to conduct the evaluation, it was important to help the agencies link the social problem, their programming, and the intended outcomes. This process also helped move away from blaming and labeling to problem solving by using language to construct a different social reality.

Understanding the problem is a requisite condition in the process of problem solving. Neither the grantor nor the grantee had a clear grasp of the problem, nor of the causal conditions that created the problem. The social problem as identified in social science research is multifaceted. The logic is that there is a need for adult guidance for healthy youth development during the transition from childhood to adulthood. The social scientists point out that during this stage youth develop habits and values that are lifelong (Dryfoos, 1990). This is also a period in human development in which curiosity, creativity, and energy levels are very high. These factors make it imperative that youth have adults involved in their lives to guide them in making choices during this critical developmental stage. Research shows that guidance from caring adults during this stage can make a difference in the life choices youth make now and will make later in life. The fact that many youth do not have supervision and nurturing from caring adults means that they will make the transition to adulthood ill-equipped for personal development and growth, work, family life, and full participation in our democratic society (Carnegie, 1995).

Given the current societal conditions, the grantor and grantee in this evaluation were asked to reconsider what is meant by at-risk and how they could best serve the interest of the youth. Obviously a grantor who is awarding small grants of $20,000 per grantee cannot expect an agency to reduce teen pregnancy in a community by 50 percent. If the agency dedicated its entire budget to this cause, it would not have any effect on the systematic problems that cause the condition to exist. Therefore, in the next funding cycle two things were done. One, the funding agency was asked to rewrite its request for proposals and to eliminate the term at-risk youth. Although the term at-risk is still used in the grantor literature, a definition is provided. The grantor working definition of at-risk was "youth who may be at risk of not making the transition from childhood to adulthood equipped to meet the adult responsibilities required for personal growth and development, work, family life, and full participation in society."

Although not perfect, the definition did provide some clarity about what factors made the youth at risk and the future consequences. The next step was to work with the grantor in developing realistic objectives for the youth initiatives. The question was what they could expect agencies to do to decrease the youth's susceptibility to the lack of preparation for adulthood. The four initiative goals for the second funding cycle were to provide funding to support agencies that:

- Provide a safe environment to engage youth in productive activities supervised by adults during the nonschool hours
- Provide activities that contribute to healthy social, psychological, and emotional youth development
- Include parents in programming as much as it is feasible to do so
- Work with other agencies to create a youth services collaborative that integrate youth social services with nontraditional youth programming

The grantor targeted youth who are parents and youth who are involved in the courts (incarcerated in juvenile detention or on probation) as priorities. These goals are broad enough to allow grantees flexibility in designing their programs.

The corresponding objectives are to increase:

- The development of life skills
- Youth self-confidence
- Youth self-esteem
- The youth's perception of personal efficacy.

Baseline and exit measures are taken for each of these variables. Additionally, process data are collected on the types of activities, the environment, the attitudes and behaviors of adults working with the youth, and the involvement of parents.

Grantees are now placing more emphasis on programming that will result in the stated initiative objectives. Most have dropped the label at-risk and instead used the simple concept of "youth programming" to define the program emphasis. The programs engage youth in activities that develop life skills such as the ability to work in a group, the ability to take responsibility for success as well as failure, the ability to receive and give honest feedback, the ability to make independent decisions, and the ability to develop and maintain meaningful relationships. The youth also receive recognition for their accomplishments and other sources of validation of their worth as individuals. Through participation in group activities, the youth develop trusting meaningful relationships with their peers and adults. Since group membership is very important to this age group, the sense of belonging to a meaningful group is one of the strongest points of the youth programs.

As the initiative begins its fourth funding cycle, the grantor agency is placing more emphasis on prevention. The criteria for evaluating the program are clearer. Data are being systematically gathered on all of the key program outcome variables to be used in an impact evaluation of the imitative.

## Language Does Matter in Evaluation

Power to coin language to describe social phenomena is variably distributed among the intellectual elite, policymakers, evaluators, and service providers. From a sociopolitical perspective, one social class has almost exclusive power to decide the contextual meaning of terms and concepts that describe social problems. In this evaluation the sociopolitical use of at-risk led to poor translation of its meaning in intergroup communication across the five groups: social scientists, policymakers, grantor agency, grantee agencies, and the youth. In this case the sociopolitical nature of the language inhibited the development of authentic programming that would meaningfully address the problem. The grantees, overwhelmed by the social reality imposed by the language of at-risk, could not conceive of overcoming the insurmountable problems.

The challenge for the evaluator was to translate the language of the social problem into measurable program outcomes for the grantor and grantee. This exercise made the agencies aware of the need to establish realistic outcomes. Changes in the language led to changes in the emphasis of the program. One, the concept shifted from at-risk youth to healthy youth development. Two, the shift in language provided an opportunity for the grantee agencies to begin to identify attributes of healthy development and to identify ways to promote healthy development. There is no doubt the political institutions will continue to use the language of at-risk. However, in this one state, its interpretation at the grantor and grantee levels will switch to the more positive language of promoting healthy youth development.

## References

Baizerman, M., and Compton, D. "From Respondent and Informant to Consultant and Participant: The Evolution of a State Agency Policy Evaluation." In A. M. Madison (ed.), *Minority Issues in Program Evaluation.* New Directions for Program Evaluation, no. 53. San Francisco: Jossey-Bass, 1992.

Bonvillain, N. *Language, Culture, and Communication: The Meaning of Messages.* Upper Saddle River, N.J.: Prentice Hall, 1993.

Bugarski, R. "Applied Linguistics as Linguistics Applied." In O. M. Tomic and R. W. Shuy (eds.), *The Relationship of Theoretical and Applied Linguistics.* San Francisco: Jossey-Bass, 1989.

Carnegie Corporation. "A Matter of Time: Risk and Opportunities in Nonschool Hours." *A Report of the Task Force on Youth Development and Community Programs.* Carnegie Corporation: New York, 1992.

Carnegie Corporation. "Great Transitions: Preparing Adolescents for a New Century." *Concluding Report of the Carnegie Council on Adolescent Development.* Carnegie Corporation: New York, 1995.

Dryfoos, J. G. *Adolescents at Risk: Prevalence and Prevention.* New York: Oxford University Press, 1990.

Edwards, J. *Language, Society, and Identity.* New York: Oxford University Press, 1985.

Feldman, S. S., and Elliott, G. R. (eds.). *At the Threshold: The Developing Adolescent.* Cambridge, Mass.: Harvard University Press, 1990.

Gumperz, J. J. (ed.). *Language and Social Identity.* New York: Cambridge University Press; 1982.

Gumperz, J. J., and Gumperz, J. C. "Language and the 'Communication of Social Identity.'" In J. J. Gumperz (ed.), *Language and Social Identity.* New York: Cambridge University Press, 1982.

Guy, G. "Language and Social Class." In F. J. Newmeyer (ed.), *Language: The Socio-Cultural Context.* New York: Cambridge University Press, 1988.

Halliday, M.A.K. (ed.). *Language as Social Semiotic.* Baltimore, Md.: University Park Press, 1978.

Halliday, M.A.K., and Hasan, R. *Language, Context, and Text: Aspects of Language in a Social-Semiotic Perspective.* New York: Oxford University Press, 1978.

Jessor, R. "Successful Adolescent Development Among Youth in High-Risk Settings." *American Psychologist,* 1993, *48* (2), 117–126.

Lele, J. K., and Singh, R. *Language and Society.* New York: E. J. Brill, 1989.

Newmeyer, F. J. (ed.). *Language: The Socio-Cultural Context.* New York: Cambridge University Press, 1988.

Pennycook, A. *The Cultural Politics of English as an International Language.* New York: Longman Press, 1994.

Schorr, L. B., and Schorr, D. *Within Our Reach: Breaking the Cycle of Disadvantage.* New York: Doubleday, 1989.

Shadish, W. R., Cook, T. D., and Leviton, L. C. *Foundations of Program Evaluation: Theories and Practice.* Thousand Oaks, Calif.: Sage, 1991.

Shapiro, M. J. *Language and Political Understanding: The Politics of Discursive Practices.* New Haven, Conn.: Yale University Press, 1981.

St. Clair, R. N. "The Contexts of Language." In R. N. St. Clair and H. Giles (eds.), *The Social and Psychological Contexts of Language.* Hillsdale, N.J.: Lawrence Erlbaum Associates, 1980.

St. Clair, R. N., and Giles, H. (eds.). *The Social and Psychological Contexts of Language.* Hillsdale, N.J.: Lawrence Erlbaum Associates, 1980.

Stufflebeam, D. "Empowerment Evaluation, Objectivist Evaluation, and Evaluation Standards: Where the Future of Evaluation Should Go and Where It Should Not Go." *Evaluation Practice,* 1994, 15 (3), 321–338.

Tomic, O. M., and Shuy, R. W. (eds.). *The Relationship of Theoretical and Applied Linguistics.* San Francisco: Jossey-Bass, 1989.

Werner, E., and Smith, R. *Overcoming the Odds: High Risk Children from Birth to Adulthood.* Ithaca, N.Y.: Cornell University Press, 1992.

*ANNA MARIE MADISON is associate professor in the College of Public and Community Service, Graduate Program in Human Services at the University of Massachusetts, Boston. She is currently the evaluator of youth development in the arts and in sustainable agriculture programs in the Commonwealth of Massachusetts and of an HIV/AIDS prevention community planning effort in Boston.*

**3**

*A sociolinguistic analysis of program beneficiaries talk in
a community-based disease prevention and intervention
program is described, including discussion of implications
for examining and understanding language in evaluation.*

# HIV/AIDS Talk: Implications for Prevention Intervention and Evaluation

*Rodney K. Hopson, Kenya J. Lucas, James A. Peterson*

> The process has gone terribly awry. . . . The undaunted search for
> quick-fix models forces us to crawl into very narrow boxes. . . . It
> jeopardizes our ability to see the world as it is, as well as our ability
> to offer constructive ideas about how to change it. In my experience,
> such models inevitably end up trying to fit the subject to the tech-
> nology, rather than the other way around. Such a procedure is rem-
> iniscent of the colonialism of an earlier age, in that these models
> become tools of abuse and neglect, rather than ones that bring com-
> fort and relief. They lead us down conceptual paths that have little
> or no relevance to the way people actually live, and hence inevitably
> to strategies and policies that have no efficacy in terms of preven-
> tion. Still worse, they fuel the metaphors of blame that already char-
> acterize the representation of those with this disease, a fact that can
> only exacerbate the suffering they experience from it [Clatts, 1994].

Reflecting on ten years of AIDS prevention research, Michael Clatts's thoughts
and admonition signal a problem in developing and evaluating culturally
appropriate HIV/AIDS prevention interventions at the cusp of the third decade
of the epidemic. The essence of Clatts's critique, which is particularly relevant

The authors acknowledge the invaluable support of Mike Agar for his ethnographic and
editorial insights and Carl Latkin for his vision of the Data Operating Center at the Light
House. A similar version of this chapter was presented at the annual meeting of the Society for Applied Anthropology, San Juan, Puerto Rico, May 1998, with funding support
from the National Institute for Drug Abuse.

for the evaluator, suggests that theory, methods, and/or practice geared toward understanding populations and beneficiaries often do not. Instead, these tools or conceptual frameworks limit what we (as researchers, and evaluators in this case) need to know; even more problematic, our own tools may *guarantee* that we will not find out what we need to know.

Significant recent work by those within the evaluation community (Chelimsky, 1998; Mertens, 1999; Ryan and others, 1998; Weiss, 1998) has been directed toward greater inclusiveness in and participatory styles of evaluation, especially where socially marginalized groups are concerned. The hallmark of an inclusive approach to evaluation, as Mertens discusses, "involves a systematic investigation of the merit or worth of a program or system, for the purpose of reducing uncertainty in decision making, and to facilitate positive social change for the least advantaged" (1999). According to those who espouse inclusiveness, struggling with issues of oppression and discrimination ought to be front and center for the evaluator. We ought to give voice to those who have been ignored in the traditional evaluation process and find a way to listen to the least powerful and the disenfranchised. Ultimately, better listening by the evaluation researcher promotes more credible information about programs and interventions.

Certainly, inclusive approaches and participatory styles of evaluation may be necessary in HIV/AIDS prevention in understanding and valuing what the disease means to those affected and inflicted. Still, however, these approaches may not be sufficient by themselves. There is no guarantee, inclusive approaches or not, that we evaluators will understand what these very marginalized beneficiaries or groups say or mean nor that we are competent or self-conscious enough to decipher the implicit and explicit messages we gather. Only part of the key lies in listening to what program people say and maintaining contact with these same people during the whole program (Weiss, 1998); another key may lie in understanding the language of the group or program people we intend to impact.

The purpose of this chapter is twofold: (1) to examine the HIV/AIDS language and meanings of former and current drug-using participants in a community-based disease prevention and intervention program, and (2) to reveal how the participants' language and meanings contributed to the design of an HIV/AIDS program intervention.

A considerable and increasing number of applied anthropologists and social scientists have contributed to understanding the sociocultural and political context of HIV/AIDS among drug users (injection and noninjection), particularly in the second decade of the epidemic (Clatts, 1994; Newmeyer, Feldman, Biernacki, and Watters, 1989; O'Connor and Leap, 1993; Singer and others, 1992). Yet little to no work, with the exception of William Leap's contribution, explores sociolinguistic analysis in understanding the context of HIV/AIDS prevention and intervention. This chapter furthers Leap's sociolinguistic analysis and encourages evaluation and program planners to consider the language of involved participants in their social context for the purposes of sustaining programs and empowering communities. Language meanings surrounding HIV/AIDS talk can provide key clues for deeper analysis of HIV-infected and -affected individuals, their related experiences and social realities, as well as for planning, implementing, and evaluating prevention intervention programs.

When language meanings of program beneficiaries reveal how they align or perceive themselves in the context of HIV/AIDS, evaluation and program planners might use this to structure more valid instruments or design interventions that are appropriate and meaningful. By linking language and HIV/AIDS, this chapter upholds the need for inclusive theories and approaches to evaluation and offers a way for evaluators to give voice to marginalized groups by analyzing the language of program participants and using their language and social meanings to direct discussions about program prevention and intervention improvement.

The chapter is divided into several sections. A conceptual framework follows to provide a sample of the bodies of knowledge that drive this work, primarily sociolinguistic, critical, and ethnographic theories. The next section describes the methods and data collection strategies, followed by an analysis of "language themes" that surfaced among program participants. The chapter concludes by offering some of the implications of paying attention to understanding language *in* evaluation.

## Conceptual Framework

> The key to understanding language in context is to start, not with language, but with context [Hymes, 1972].

Two presuppositions naturally drive the conceptual framework of this chapter. First, the language and meaning that program participants assign to their knowledge of HIV/AIDS and the knowledge of the social world in which they live are important precepts in designing, implementing, and evaluating appropriate public health intervention strategies. Second, understanding how drug-using groups construct their social reality is inextricably linked with the words, concepts, and language patterns they use to reveal cultural meanings and norms (Berger and Luckmann, 1967; Bonvillain, 1993; Whorf, 1956).

Attention to the ways that affected participants talk and think about HIV/AIDS requires consideration of the larger social and professional discourse on the disease. It is through framing this larger social discourse and context where we begin to pay heed to Dell Hymes's thought about language in its social context. Hymes (1972) understood, for instance, concerning the functions of language in the classroom, that participants (learners) brought with them community and social norms of speaking into their learning environments. These community and social norms were vital in deciphering the language they brought to school. It was not so much "culturally deficient" as it was "culturally different," and the task for the teacher was in making sense of this difference, without stereotyping the learner (and his or her community) into a host of pathologies. In his seminal paper, Hymes argues that

> what we need to know goes far beyond how the grammar of English is organized as something to be taught. It has to do with the relationship between a grammar of English and the ways in which English is organized in use by teachers, by children, and by the communities from which they come . . . in short, with the relation of the structure of language to the structure of speaking [Hymes, 1972].

Mike Agar's notion of languaculture (1994 and depicted in the final chapter of this volume) reinforces the role of language in its sociocultural context. To Agar, communicating involves more than understanding grammar and using a dictionary, which he refers to as "language in a circle." His work reveals the need to consider the importance of language and cultural differences in communication and conversation, and the inextricable link between language and culture. He observes, "Language fills the space between us with sound; culture forges the human connection through them. Culture is in language, and language is loaded with culture." Both Hymes and Agar thus suggest that language, culture, and human thinking are linked. The extent to which the words available in a language influence people's perceptions of their world is further exemplified in the divide that surfaces around the social and cultural meanings of HIV/AIDS.

**The Social Discourse of HIV/AIDS.** That the discourse surrounding AIDS during the first two decades of the epidemic was characterized, in Paul Farmer and Arthur Kleinman's view (1989), as "the rational-technical language of disease control" is a fitting societal depiction of the disease. The social construction of the disease has been likened to other illnesses that have become "icons of the times . . . in its capacity to menace and hurt, to burden and spoil human experience, and to elicit questions about the nature of life and its significance" (1989). Like tuberculosis, leprosy, hepatitis, cholera, mental illness, and cancer (Bosk and Frader, 1991; Farmer and Kleinman, 1989; Rosenberg, 1992; White, 1988), AIDS has been framed by a series of powerful and often contradictory messages that bespeak intergenerational loss, victim-blaming, and deserved punishment (Bosk and Frader, 1991; Payne and Risch, 1984). These meanings, as Charles Rosenberg points out (1992), are driven by the public's penetrating view of the disease, one that contrasted with the medical profession's views and discoveries:

> The meaning of scientific knowledge is determined by its consumers. When certain immunologists suggest that predisposition to AIDS may grow out of successive onslaughts on the immune system, it may or may not prove to be

an accurate description of the natural world. As with the case with cholera a century and a half before, the emphasis on repeated infections explains how a person with AIDS had "predisposed" himself or herself. The meaning lies in behavior uncontrolled. When an epidemiologist notes that the incidence of AIDS correlates with numbers of sexual contacts, he may be speaking in terms of likelihoods; to many of his fellow Americans he is speaking of guilt and deserved punishment [Rosenberg, 1992].

These conflicting views held by the general public and those by medical scientists seem to be particularly vivid, considering the scientific knowledge and technological expertise of this Western culture. Amidst the huge number of legal cases that redefined social institutions, constitutional principles, and personal relationships in our American society as a result of the AIDS epidemic (Gostin, 1990), the first decade can be characterized by an absence of federal government assistance for localities planning for the burden of providing HIV/AIDS care, a lack of commitment to drug treatment, and the declining support for social programs (Bayer, 1992). Ostensibly, the hegemonic public view of AIDS that associated the disease with an underclass and unwanted population underlies these policy trends. Farmer and Kleinman (1989) suggest:

> There is the moral meaning of shame and humiliation imposed by the very commercialized culture that made money from the images of sexuality and drugs: now these same images have been transformed, rationally but still hypocritically (since money is still to be made from the meanings), from desires into risks.

As the public image of the disease was directed toward blaming individuals, communities, and "risk groups," most vulnerable groups were silent and either denied or refused assistance. Renee Sabatier (1988) suggested that victim-blaming also diverted attention away from direct aid and toward more systemic problems, in this case researching the disease, finding a cure, and encouraging communities to respond to the epidemic. Using the black community as an example, Harlon Dalton and others (Quimby, 1992) contend that lack of reaction and direct response to the disease was not so much a lack of willingness to address the issue or refusal to adhere to what Farmer and Kleinman term a powerful cultural premise in North American society: "the concept of autonomous individuals who are solely responsible for their fate, including their illness" (1989). Instead, Dalton describes this inactivity and nonacceptance as "the predictable outgrowth of the problematic relationship between the black community and the larger society, a relationship characterized by domination and subordination, mutual fear and mutual respect, a sense of otherness and a pervasive neglect that rarely feels benign" (1989). Quimby, moreover, points to a plethora of factors that influenced African-American responses to AIDS (1992), such as reflections of white denial, dominant political hesitancy from both black and white leadership, and inappropriate public health education.

**Framing Alternative Discourse and Language.** Faced with daunting tasks to pursue HIV prevention research, applied social scientists such as Quimby point to a need to increase the hearing of alternative voices, to conduct empowering research, and to ground cultural representations of groups being studied into interdisciplinary work. Leap's (1990) sociolinguistic work on language, meaning, and AIDS is an important step in coming to terms with these voices and cultural representations of groups. Leap shows that speakers, consciously or not, provide clues about their point of view about AIDS and their relationship to the disease. He posits that

> language choices contribute to the creation of meaning and the exchange of meaning within particular social settings. The action here is ongoing on two levels: there is meaning which grows out of the speakers' *use* of language (e.g. the selection of words and phrases, choices between options in grammar and style). And there is also meaning within the structure of language itself, whose influence on conversation and communication the speaker may be able either to highlight or to mask, but will never be able completely to submerge.

Perhaps what Leap does most deliberately is to provide a conceptual avenue for the interdisciplinary study of language and AIDS. Hence, his work constitutes "the beginnings of what can become a profile of *expectable language usage* whenever speakers of American English talk about AIDS" (1990), and is valuable to the evaluation community as we seek to understand diverse HIV/AIDS meanings.

Laura Smith, Kenya Lucas, and Carl Latkin, in their preliminary examination of rumor and gossip about HIV and AIDS, are important insofar as they reveal that messages from participants are useful in informing the context of HIV prevention during the design phase of a program (1999). In paying attention to this particular social discourse on HIV/AIDS, Smith and others contribute to Leap's discussion on language and argument that HIV/AIDS prevention efforts target social networks rather than individuals. Their work underscores the need to pay attention to the sociolinguistic detail of program beneficiaries and community members for design and intervention purposes.

## Data Collection: Summary and Analysis

Since 1996, the Self Help through Intervention and Prevention (SHIPS) Studies has been located at the Light House, an off-campus research facility of the department of Health Policy and Management at the Johns Hopkins University School of Hygiene and Public Health. Building on a community-based, interdisciplinary research program, the Light House's SHIPS studies have initiated a number of projects, primarily focusing on disease prevention and health promotion among minority and poor populations in the city of Baltimore.

Data for this analysis were drawn from two of the Light House projects, Self Help in Eliminating Life-Threatening Diseases (SHIELD) and Social Affiliates in Injectors' Lives (SAIL) during their initial three-year funding periods by the National Institute on Drug Abuse (NIDA). SHIELD has since been funded for an additional three-year period. The SHIELD project, a sociobehavioral HIV/AIDS intervention study, uses an experimental design to examine the feasibility and efficacy of training individuals from the drug-using community to become health educators and to promote HIV prevention and risk reduction within their social networks. An ethnographic portion of the SHIELD research design was implemented to provide rich contextual information about the community domain, augment the quantitative data derived from interviews, and help encode views of drug-using participants. SAIL's goals were twofold: to identify the role of family as support resource in maintaining and adopting HIV risk reduction strategies for high risk individuals, and to assess the association between the HIV-infected person's drug relapse and processes of coping.

**Methods.** Ethnographic interviews, ranging between seventy-five and ninety minutes in length, were conducted with seventy-five recruited HIV-infected and -affected men and women of the two projects, SHIELD and SAIL, from middle of 1996 to the end of 1997. Forty participants of the SHIELD project completed the first wave of a semistructured, informal qualitative interview that surveyed a number of issues designed to examine the participants' behaviors in their social context. These issues included questions about their sociodemographics, daily routine, drug-use profile, knowledge of HIV/AIDS risks, drug and sexual sociobehavioral characteristics, and talk about HIV/AIDS. Thirty-five participants of the SAIL study completed an open-ended qualitative interview that explored themes related to perceptions and meanings assigned to HIV/AIDS, how the disease was affecting them and their support systems, and other discourse and attitudes surrounding the disease.

**Results.** Consistent with the work of James Spradley (1979), ethnographic data provided background information concerning how interviewees assigned meaning to HIV/AIDS in their lives. Building on the sociolinguistic work of Leap (1990), emphasis was placed on generating a set of language themes and categories that evolved out of the conversations and narratives of the SHIELD and SAIL participants. The analysis attempted to provide project staff with a lens to see how the HIV-infected and -affected people frame their lives and come to terms with the disease for future prevention intervention and evaluation activities.

As depicted in Table 3.1, a number of themes and their respective central issues serve as parameters for understanding conceptions of HIV/AIDS of the program participants. The ten generated language themes furthermore provide the basis for knowledge of HIV/AIDS in an urban, predominantly

### Table 3.1. HIV/AIDS Language Themes and Central Issues

| Language Themes[1] | Central Issues |
|---|---|
| Blame | • association of responsibility for HIV/AIDS origins, transmissions, causes, and so on<br>• outcome of interplay between one's view about HIV/AIDS causes and politics of issue |
| Ownership | • HIV/AIDS as perceived property<br>• HIV/AIDS as legitimate concern/problem for individual or group |
| Acceptance (or nonacceptance) | • expression of ownership, association, and/or blame<br>• emancipatory or oppressive connotations |
| Abbreviations | • symbols with respect to HIV/AIDS meaning construct |
| References (to positive status) | • identification of HIV-positive as articulation of what it means to be infected<br>• ideological marker that distinguishes self from infected/uninfected |
| (Verb) references | • how individuals act in relation to HIV/AIDS |
| (Pronoun) references (for example, "us" versus "them") | • how one aligns/relates to others in terms of HIV/AIDS issue |
| Self-identification | • how individuals identify themselves in context of HIV/AIDS issue |
| Synonyms | • terms used interchangeably with HIV/AIDS |
| Labeling | • process of HIV/AIDS social definition<br>• influence of social politics and societal values in understanding HIV/AIDS |

[1]In the table, macro-level conceptions consist of blame, ownership, and acceptance themes. Micro-level conceptions consist of abbreviations, synonyms, referencing, self-identification, and labeling themes.

African-American context so that relevant interventions and preventions may be conceptualized. Table 3.1 asserts that relative to the participants' use and structure of language surrounding HIV/AIDS, two separate categories of themes emerged. One set of themes characterized the larger and macro-level conception of the disease, and the second set of themes represented an individual perspective or micro level of the disease. Several noteworthy examples are illustrated below, followed by a discussion about the implications for HIV/AIDS prevention and how the intervention was improved by understanding and incorporating language themes.

Within the macro-level conception reverberated issues such as respondents' association of responsibility for HIV/AIDS origins, transmissions, and causes (blame), and the recognition of HIV/AIDS as perceived property for a particular individual or group (ownership). For example, one participant described what he perceived as blame and ownership related to the disease in the following:

I think everything is come across seas myself. I think the diseases is comin' across seas . . . I think over in Ethiop–, what do you call it, Ethiopia. Somewhere or over there where they be havin' them bombs at, you know, with the war and all that. Or, I'm not gonna say where. Anybody can have it on 'em. . . . It wasn't in the United States until what, ten, fifteen years ago? Something like that? Back in '85?, '84? Who brought it over here? That what I wanna know. . . . I'm still tryin' to find out where it came from but they don't know. People bring things from overseas over here. Fifteen or twenty years ago you didn't hear about no AIDS in the United States. Now you got it 'cause people from across seas come over here with it. The Koreans, the Russians, uh, Spanish. You got all different kinds of cultures just comin' over here and bringing disease off the boat that they didn't never know nothin' about. And now it's a worldwide disease. It's the main killer in the world, am I wrong? So they need to do something about it. People just droppin' like flies, that don't make no sense. Don't make no sense at all [SHIELD 2072:454:506/747:787].

Drug-using subcultures do not exist in isolation; they consume the same medical and popular knowledge as that which shape norms and beliefs about the origin and cause of HIV/AIDS in the larger society. Furthermore, the politics of excluding oneself or one's group from blame for the epidemic demand that others who do not share identities (though they may share disadvantage—as in the case of marginalized immigrants) are scapegoated. This reactive groupness or oppositional culture reshapes the landscape of blame at the macro level, further promoting divisive and combative discourse that (as previously mentioned) ultimately shapes HIV/AIDS program design and program implementation. The three emergent issues at the macro level thus signal a number of reasons for reluctance to "own" HIV/AIDS for members of communities that have become most profoundly affected by the disease.

Regarding the micro-level conception, more direct references to the disease and meanings of the disease at a personal level were manifest. This is implied by how participants, for instance, aligned themselves in terms of the issues (referencing), reacted to the social definition of HIV/AIDS (labeling), or articulated what it meant to be affected or afflicted with the disease (references to positive status). An example of disease labeling is manifest in one participant's description of the social definition of HIV/AIDS:

And up until I came into the program, I didn't know anybody with AIDS. I . . . thought that AIDS was nothing but a junkie, a prostitute disease. You were like no good living on the street or trash. And today . . . I know doctors and lawyers with it. It just doesn't discriminate. It's just like that disease of addiction (Interviewer: So, how did you get that image in your mind that that was what people . . .) That's how I was raised. White is good; black is bad. You grow prejudice; you grow narrow-minded. You know, backward type of people [SHIELD 2109:300–312].

How participants who are affected or infected by HIV/AIDS self-identify with the disease is another important language theme. How individuals perceive themselves in context of the disease (identity formulation) is shaped by important cultural aspects and models. Elisa Sobo's (1997, 1999) work on this issue helps situate self-disclosure meaning and underscores the importance of framing cultural models for AIDS intervention and evaluation. The following quote is illustrative of how participants associate themselves:

> I go to see my doctors . . . professionals and talk about it and I cry about it because sometimes for real HIV [is] the least of my problems, but sometimes I wake up and I don't want it, you know. I wake up and I don't want to be an addict, or I wake up and I don't want to be HIV-positive, and sometimes when I go through those kind of changes I go to my doctors [SAIL0001:101:161].

An additional theme concerning how participants use or structure language around HIV/AIDS is through their direct referencing of the disease, or in Leap's view how "speakers use language to establish their sense of self, as actor and/or observer within AIDS related social domains" (1990). Our analysis, consistent with Leap's, found similar referencing options: choice of verb reference and choice of personal pronoun reference. An illustration of verb-referencing is included below:

> But I never did drink behind anybody anyway. But I really don't at all now. If they ain't—I'm drinking something that they ain't, I don't even let them have it. I don't give them none. I mean you probably can't catch it behind drinking, I guess. I don't know for sure. But I think you might can catch it behind it. So, you can catch a cold behind people who drink something, so it's basically almost a germ, so you probably can catch it like that. But I don't know [SHIELD2221:895–912].

Verb referencing, in the above, is manifested in the speaker's relationship with the acquisition of AIDS. His reference to how he can "catch" AIDS signals that the acquisition of the disease may be out of his control, as though the disease transmission can be initiated without his own involvement and action. Leap suggests that "the *source* of the illness remains at a distance from the party who ultimately encounters it when *catch* is selected as the sentence verb" (1990).

These macro- and micro-level meanings of HIV/AIDS are significant considering the import of interaction between those in the drug-using culture and service providers, the need to develop reliable and valid instruments to evaluate knowledge about HIV/AIDS, and the general schema of HIV/AIDS prevention and its implication for the biomedical and public health paradigmatic approaches to health and illness. What Tola Pearce (1993) has shown in an African context concerning medical knowledge among lay people in Nigeria is applicable here. In her article, she differentiates three factors that generate medical "facts": macro or sociocultural level (shaped by the socioeconomic context in which groups operate), intermediate level (influenced by the medical sector that has a combination of Western and indigenous remedies), and the individual or micro level (derived from personal experiences and subculture). To Pearce, how medical "facts" are generated by the public and how these facts are related to other aspects of Yoruba culture are a worthy study, particularly considering Berger and Luckmann's (1967) claim that our perception of reality is socially constructed as persons go about solving problems of everyday life. Because "individuals thus accumulate a repertoire of information relevant to their various domains of activity" (Pearce, 1993), this information can serve the basis for understanding how groups and subcultures make sense of health and disease.

## Implications for HIV/AIDS Prevention: Understanding Language in Evaluation

At the end of this second decade of the HIV/AIDS epidemic, those in the applied evaluation discipline together with other public health professionals have an opportunity to rethink theory and approach methods that are driven by the meanings, experiences, and language of target populations. Inherent in the way participants in HIV/AIDS prevention and intervention programs talk about disease are the complex meanings that grow out of their language use and structure. These language meanings, in turn, provide key clues for deeper analysis of participants' experiences, life histories, and profiles.

In the case of the language meaning data collected from the ethnographic interviews, results were useful in the further design and improvement of the prevention intervention program. Specifically, the language-sensitive data were valuable in the design of an ethnographic intervention model developed to help ground the larger intervention in a holistic awareness of the local context and its impact on drug-user beliefs and behaviors. One element of this intervention model focused on the language meanings related to ways of conceiving HIV/AIDS (Hopson, Peterson, Lucas, forthcoming). Thus, these language themes helped "build a picture of the social world of the drug-addicted and diseased in the inner city as a means toward the design of appropriate HIV/AIDS intervention and drugs research."

The language meanings were furthermore valuable in the design of the post-intervention instrument. Concepts and questions elicited during the ethnographic interview formed the basis for refining and assessing the appropriateness of follow-up questionnaires, both quantitative and qualitative (Peterson, Agar, Latkin, 1999). For instance, subsequent interviews contained items reflecting HIV/AIDS talk (who have you talked with about HIV/AIDS recently, what did you talk about, and so on) largely believed to focus on initiating change more at the social network than the individual level.

Current trends in the evaluation discipline emphasize inclusive and empowerment approaches to evaluation (Chelimsky, 1998; Fetterman, Kaftarian, and Wandersman, 1996; Mertens, 1999; Ryan and others, 1998). That is, evaluators can frame more useful evaluations by listening to the voices of real people and acting on what program people say, as in the case of empowerment evaluation (Mayer, 1996). And in the case of inclusive strategies, evaluators can do more to encourage local participation and democratically produced information and data. These innovative and timely approaches to evaluation require too that we understand the languages that stakeholders, beneficiaries, and others whom we intend to empower or democratize. We must understand how they construct their social context and world amid the problems and challenges that await them. Language *in* evaluation assumes that *we empower ourselves* with understanding cultural models and meanings and the means by which groups and individuals frame the world in which they interact and live, and that we ensure our program instrumentation and content reflect more these models and meanings than our own. Through understanding existing languages, our prevention intervention and evaluation work can be more contextually relevant and effective.

## References

Agar, M. H. *Language Shock: Understanding the Culture of Conversation.* New York: William Morrow and Company, 1994.

Bayer, R. "Entering the Second Decade: The Politics of Prevention, the Politics of Neglect." In E. Fee and D. M. Fox (eds.), *AIDS: The Making of a Chronic Disease.* Berkeley, Calif.: University of California Press, 1992.

Berger, P. L., and Luckmann, T. *The Social Construction of Reality: A Treatise in the Sociology of Knowledge.* New York: Anchor Books, 1967.

Bonvillain, N. *Language, Culture, and Communication: The Meaning of Messages.* Upper Saddle River, N.J.: Prentice-Hall, 1993.

Bosk, C. L., and Frader, J. E. "AIDS and Its Impact on Medial Work: The Culture and Politics of the Shop Floor." In D. Nelkin, D. P. Willis, and S. V. Parris (eds.), *A Disease of Society: Cultural and Institutional Responses to AIDS.* Cambridge, United Kingdom: Cambridge University Press, 1991.

Chelimsky, E. "The Role of Experience in Formulating Theories of Evaluation Practice." *American Journal of Evaluation,* 1998, *19*(1), 21–34.

Clatts, M. C. "All the King's Horses and the All the King's Men: Some Personal Reflections on Ten Years of AIDS Ethnography." *Human Organization,* 1994, *53* (1), 93–95.

Dalton, H. "AIDS as Blackface." *Daedalus,* 1989, *118,* 205–226.

Farmer, P., and Kleinman, A. "AIDS as Human Suffering." *Daedalus,* 1989, *118,* 135–162.

Fetterman, D. M., Kaftarian, S. J., and Wandersman, A. (eds.). *Empowerment Evaluation: Knowledge and Tools for Self-Assessment and Accountability.* Thousand Oaks, Calif.: Sage, 1996.

Gostin, L. O. "The AIDS Litigation Project." *Journal of the American Medical Association,* 1990, *263* (14), 1961–1970.

Hopson, R. K., Peterson, J. A., and Lucas, K. J. "Tales from the 'Hood': Framing HIV/AIDS Prevention Through Intervention Ethnography in the Inner City." In T. Rhodes and D. Moore (eds.), *Qualitative Research in the Addictions.* Addictions Research, forthcoming.

Hymes, D. Introduction in C. B. Cazden, V. P. John, and D. Hymes (eds.), *Functions of Language in the Classroom.* New York: Columbia University Teacher's College, 1972.

Leap, W. "Language and AIDS." In D. Feldman (ed.), *Culture and AIDS.* New York: Praeger, 1990.

Mayer, S. E. "Building Community Capacity with Evaluation Activities That Empower." In D. M. Fetterman, S. J. Kaftarian, and A. Wandersman (eds.), *Empowerment Evaluation: Knowledge and Tools for Self-Assessment and Accountability.* Thousand Oaks, Calif.: Sage, 1996.

Mertens, D. M. "Inclusive Evaluation: Implications of Transformative Theory for Evaluation." *American Journal of Evaluation,* 1999, *20*(1), 1–14.

Newmeyer, J. A., Feldman, H. W., Biernacki, P., and Watters, J. K. "Preventing AIDS Contagion Among Intravenous Drug Users." *Medical Anthropology,* 1989, *10,* 167–175.

O'Connor, K. A., and Leap, W. (eds.). "AIDS Outreach, Education, and Prevention: Anthropological Contributions." *Practicing Anthropology,* 1993, *15*(4).

Payne, K. W., and Risch, S. J. "The Politics of AIDS: Homophobia, Medicine, and Public Health." *Science for the People,* 1984, *16,* 17–24.

Pearce, T. O. "Lay Medical Knowledge in an African Context." In S. Lindenbaum and M. Lock, *Knowledge, Power, and Practice: The Anthropology of Medicine in Everyday Life.* Berkeley, Calif.: University of California Press, 1993.

Peterson, J., Agar, M., and Latkin, C. "Making the Link: Triangulating HIV/AIDS Intervention Evaluation Methods." Paper presented at the Society for the Applied Anthropology annual conference, Tucson, Ariz., 1999.

Quimby, E. "Anthropological Witnessing for African-Americans: Power, Responsibility, and Choice in the Age of AIDS." In G. Herdt and S. Lindenbaum (eds.), *The Time of AIDS: Social Analysis, Theory, and Method.* Thousand Oaks, Calif.: Sage, 1992.

Rosenberg, C. E. "Disease and Social Order in America: Perceptions and Expectations." In E. Fee and D. M. Fox (eds.), *AIDS: The Burdens of History.* Berkeley, Calif.: University of California Press, 1992.

Ryan, K., and others. *American Journal of Evaluation,* 1998, *19*(1), 101–122.

Sabatier, R. "AIDS and Race: Why It Matters." In J. Tinker (ed.), *Blaming Others: Prejudice, Race, and Worldwide AIDS.* Washington, D.C.: The Panos Institute, 1988.

Singer, M., and others. "AIDS and the IV Drug User: The Local Context in Prevention Efforts." *Medical Anthropology,* 1992, *14,* 285–306.

Smith, L. C., Lucas, K. J., and Latkin, C. "Rumor and Gossip: Social Discourse on HIV and AIDS." *Anthropology and Medicine,* 1999, *16*(1), 121–131.

Sobo, E. J. "Self-Disclosure and Self-Construction Among HIV-Positive People: The Rhetorical Uses of Stereotypes and Sex." *Anthropology and Medicine,* 1997, *4*(1), 67–87.

Sobo, E. J. "Cultural Models and HIV/AIDS: New Anthropological Views. *Anthropology and Medicine,* 1999, *6*(1), 5–12.

Spradley, J. P. *The Ethnographic Interview.* Chicago: Holt, Rinehart and Winston, 1979.

Weiss, C. H. "Have We Learned Anything New About the Use of Evaluation?" *American Journal of Evaluation,* 1998, *19* (1), 21–33.

White, E. G. *Desire of Ages.* Altamont, Tenn.: Harvestine, 1988.

Whorf, B. L. "The Relation of Habitual Thought and Behavior to Language." In J. Carol (ed.), *Language, Thought, and Reality: Selected Writings of Benjamin Lee Whorf.* Cambridge: MIT Press, 1956.

RODNEY K. HOPSON *is assistant professor of education in the Department of Foundations and Leadership, School of Education, and a faculty member in the Center for Interpretative and Qualitative Research at Duquesne University in Pittsburgh.*

KENYA J. LUCAS *is a student in the Department of Sociology in the A.M.–Ph.D. program, where her research interests lie in HIV prevention and interventions, substance abuse, urban ethnographic methodology, and applied sociolinguistics.*

JAMES A. PETERSON *is senior ethnographer for a community-based research unit in the Department of Health Policy and Management, School of Hygiene and Public Health, the Johns Hopkins University, and a doctoral candidate in the Urban Education Leadership Program with a concentration on social policy, Morgan State University.*

4

*This chapter examines the use of program evaluation findings as a tool for policy learning. It argues that program evaluation findings must be "translated" into policy language in order to affect decision making within policy communities. This translation is illustrated by welfare policy innovation in Quebec.*

# Translating Evaluation Findings into "Policy Language"

*Kenneth Cabatoff*

Program evaluation findings are an important resource for policy entrepreneurs attempting to mobilize support for new policy ideas. Formal or "scientific" program evaluation uses empirical evidence and nonpartisan values that appeal to broad segments of the policy community. By examining the results of implementation in an apparently nonpartisan way and by ensuring that policy prescriptions are based on empirical evidence, program evaluators can help bridge the gap between the ideological arguments characteristic of spontaneous evaluation and the more widely shared consensual values of the community.

It is in this sense, according to Sabatier (1988), that program evaluation and other forms of systematic policy research can promote "policy learning," conducive not only to the improvement of public policies and programs, but also to the development of political support for the improvements in question. In many cases, however, program evaluation fails to play this useful role. As Cronbach and Associates (1980, p. 84) have pointed out, evaluators too often adopt a narrow view of their intended users:

> The theory of evaluation . . . has been developed almost wholly around the image of command. It is supposed that information flows to a manager or policy official who has a firm grasp on the controls. . . . Actually, however, most action is determined by a pluralistic community, not by a lone decision maker. . . . When there are multiple participants with multiple views, it is meaningless to speak of one action as the rational or correct action. The active parties jockey toward a politically acceptable accommodation.

Evaluation methodologies developed since the 1970s have placed much greater emphasis on the evaluator's "responsibility for utilization" (Patton, 1988). Still, such "utilization-focused" approaches (Patton, 1986) usually assume some form of explicit dialogue or exchange with intended users, thus underestimating the scale and complexity of decision-making processes within policy communities.

As Chen (1990, p. 67) points out, the concerns of policy communities usually go beyond those of individual stakeholders:

> Because key stakeholders' understanding of both social problems and the theory of a program are usually based upon common sense or hunch, the construction of program theory based exclusively on the stakeholders' perspective may not be sufficiently sensitive to capture the complicated causal processes underlying the program.

The focus on individual stakeholders, according to Chen, leads to a preoccupation with too small a number of evaluation criteria. "Policy language," on the other hand, requires simultaneous attention to a broad range of evaluation criteria. In terms of the "satisficing" model proposed by Herbert Simon (Cyert, Simon, and Trow, 1971), policy communities seek solutions that are "good enough" for a broad range of actors, rather than the "best possible" solutions for a small number of actors. As Chen argues (1990, pp. 68–69):

> When an evaluation situation requires dealing with more than one basic value, the use of either the stakeholder or the social science approach is not sufficient. . . . Weiss and Bucavalas's study empirically demonstrates that decision makers use multiple scientific and political criteria rather than any single criterion in judging the usefulness of a research project.

Chen thus raises concerns similar to those of Cronbach and Associates (1980, p. 336), who argue that:

> The evaluation of one program does *not* stand alone and should not be planned as if it could. It is properly to be seen as part of the movement of social thought on a broad front. Substantial managerial changes are required to enable research to perform that broad function properly.

While Cronbach and associates favor "managerial changes" as a way of creating larger frameworks for evaluation, the present chapter suggests instead that more meaningful "translation" of evaluation language into policy languages may make program evaluation more relevant to decision making at the policy community level.

Effective translation, in this sense, would require greater awareness of the culture, background, and traditions of the policy communities being influenced, as well as of the actors and policy publics most important to decision making in those communities. Program evaluation recommendations would be framed with a view toward winning support from the actors, groups, and policy publics in question. Attempts would be made to promote processes of linguistic and conceptual innovation in order to overcome the obstacles posed by outdated and inaccurate conceptions of the problems to be dealt with. Unfortunately, most evaluation training courses provide few opportunities for developing and using such translation skills.

## Policy Communities as Organized Anarchies: The Chemistry of Policy Innovation

An important obstacle to effective use of policy research, as Sabatier has pointed out, is that most policy communities are composed of rival "advocacy coalitions" that attempt to make use of evaluation research in purely partisan ways (Sabatier, 1988; Sabatier and Jenkins-Smith, 1993). While it may be easy to win support for program evaluation recommendations within a given advocacy coalition, it will be more difficult to mobilize the same support among members of opposing advocacy coalitions. Bipartisan support requires policy proposals that can appeal simultaneously to members of several advocacy coalitions, providing few targets for potential rivals or opponents.

The ability of a new idea to win support from broad segments of a policy community has been explored by J. Kingdon and other students of "organized anarchies" (Cohen, March, and Olsen, 1972; Kingdon, 1984). According to Kingdon, the ability of a new idea to win support depends on the evolution of the "policy streams" found in the local policy community. An idea will be judged acceptable when a "coupling" has been attained among the different policy streams involved.

According to Cohen, March, and Olsen (1972) there are normally four different policy streams: the problems stream, the solutions stream, the actors stream, and the decision opportunities stream. Most of the time, these four streams evolve quite independently of one another. Decisions occur on the rather exceptional occasions when the four streams converge: that is, when a decision-making opportunity occurs at the precise moment that there are policy brokers prepared to make use of the opportunity, when there is a widely shared belief that a plausible solution has been found for a recognized problem, and when there is a conviction that the problem in question requires immediate action.

While the legitimacy of a new idea thus depends to some extent on fortuitous events—on the convergence of the four policy streams—policy entrepreneurs can and do employ strategies of persuasion, lobbying, and policy research—including program evaluation—in attempting to influence the policy streams. They try to increase the probability, in other words, that future decision-making opportunities will favor their policy ideas rather than those of their competitors.

To say that policy results from "couplings" between priority problems and plausible solutions is not to say, however, that the couplings in question are always rational or efficient. Some couplings may in fact be quite dysfunctional, especially when viewed from outside the policy community in question. Referred to by Cohen, March, and Olsen (1972) as the "garbage can model," these processes nevertheless make possible decisions that, at the time they are made, seem rational and credible to the actors involved.

Those who make policy decisions within organized anarchies are subject to multiple constraints—on time, energy, and policy-relevant information—that reduce the probability that policy innovation will be effective. As a result, policies tend to reflect the ideas already present in the policy community rather than the new ideas that might result from effective usage of program evaluation results.

By ensuring better use of the information available and by expressing this information through the "policy language" current in the policy community in question, program evaluation can help promote more realistic definitions of the problems being dealt with as well as better choices among the available policy options.

The translation of program evaluation findings into policy-relevant information is complicated, however, by the fact that individual policy communities tend to interact extensively with other policy communities, and each policy community has its own language, traditions, and professional culture (Cabatoff, 1996). Managing the exchanges between distinct policy communities thus requires some familiarity with the policy languages found in each of the communities in question.

## The "Policy Language" of Welfare Reform: An Example from Quebec

In Quebec, program evaluators have been successful in identifying the weaknesses of existing welfare policies and have provided plausible explanations for the failures of existing programs. In so doing, they have stimulated the search for more effective welfare policies and have encouraged a process of ongoing experimentation with different types of welfare-to-work programs. As a general rule, however, these evaluations have failed to generate a genuine process of policy learning.

Existing programs retain many of the deficiencies identified in previous programs, and new policy initiatives tend to repeat the errors of the old ones (Normand, 1996). This "arrested learning" (March and Olsen, 1976) seems to have resulted, at least in part, from a failure to translate the language of program evaluation into an effective policy language within the policy communities involved.

Welfare reform is complicated, in Quebec as elsewhere, by the presence of two important advocacy coalitions, each strongly opposed to the "solutions" proposed by members of the opposing coalition.

The first of these can be referred to as the economic or "neo-liberal" coalition. It includes economists and policy specialists working within the Quebec government and others working in universities and private businesses. This advocacy coalition sees welfare reform in *economic* terms: there are too many people on welfare, and the cost of supporting them is an unacceptable burden on government and on society.

Members of this coalition feel that welfare recipients should be forced, if necessary, to accept employment in private business or in government-sponsored work programs. They see the question as one of economic incentives. Better economic incentives for seeking paid employment, and fewer economic incentives for staying on welfare, can motivate welfare recipients to seek paid employment (Bellemare, 1995; Lessard, 1996).

The second advocacy coalition is the community activist or "social economy" coalition. Composed of trade union members, feminist and antipoverty groups, and political and community service organizations, this coalition sees welfare as the result of failed economic and social policies. For them, it is the lack of suitable employment opportunities, rather than the unwillingness to seek paid employment, that explains why large numbers of Quebec residents have become chronic welfare recipients. They argue that welfare-to-work programs should be linked with job-creation measures, on the grounds that there is little point in preparing welfare recipients for jobs that do not exist.

The views of the social economy coalition should not be confused with those of Marxist and libertarian groups, who are just as critical of the social economy approach as they are of traditional welfare-to-work programs. Marxists argue that the CITs, or cooperative employment companies, are just another way of forcing welfare recipients to provide "cheap labor" for capitalist business enterprises (Boivin, 1995, 1995/96). Partly because of these criticisms, the term CIT was eventually dropped altogether, to be replaced by the less controversial term *entreprises d'insertion* (reintegration companies) (Bordeleau, 1996).

The term *économie sociale,* a key term in the policy language of Quebec's welfare reform policy community, is difficult to translate into English, because of the lack of a strong social economy tradition in most English-speaking countries. This difficulty is illustrated by the title of a bilingual book on social economy published in Belgium. The French title is *Economie sociale: entre économie capitaliste et économie publique* (Defourny and Monzon Campos, 1992). The literal translation would be *The social economy: between capitalist and public economies.* But the title is actually translated as *The third sector: cooperative, mutual, and nonprofit organizations.*

Since members of the social economy coalition hold the government responsible for high unemployment rates, they are critical of punitive measures aimed at welfare recipients. In the early 1990s, for example, it was common to refer to welfare inspectors as *Boubou-macoutes* (Lessard, 1993). Boubou was a nickname for the provincial premier Robert Bourassa, while macoutes was an unflattering analogy with the security police of Haitian dictator Jean-Claude Duvalier, known as the Tonton-macoutes.

The Corporations intermédiaires du travail (cooperative employment agencies) can thus be seen as an attempt to respond to the concerns of the social economy advocacy coalition, while adopting a more aggressive approach to getting people off welfare—a policy objective traditionally identified with the economic or neo-liberal coalition.

The CITs are a way of providing welfare recipients with job experience, but also—at least in theory—a way of creating new jobs. As stated in a government document describing the CITs (Gouvernement du Québec, 1993a, p. 14, author's translation):

> The labor market cannot generate enough jobs to absorb the thousands of people laid off by industrial restructuring, as well as those who enter the labor market every year and the thousands of short-term and long-term unemployed. . . . The government must develop new economic sectors; it must contribute to job creation by organizing activities whose development would be impossible under the normal conditions of the free market.

The free market, according to the CIT's proponents, is unable to make use of the short-term and fragmented employment opportunities often found in the local economy (Gouvernement du Québec, 1993b, p. 2):

> It is well known, for example, that a market gardener is able to offer employment for only a few weeks in the summer. However, by combining the needs of several different producers, the Cooperative Employment Agency (Corporation intermédiaire du travail) can create numerous jobs by acting as a link between producers whose manpower needs, taken collectively, can extend over several months. In the same way, a cooperative employment agency can bring together the needs of several different persons eligible for home care benefits . . . who, with the support of the Ministry of Health and Social Services and the Ministry of Manpower, Income Security and Professional Training, can hire welfare recipients, who then become full-time salaried employees working on a permanent basis.

The CITs are thus a clear example of the social economy approach (Barreto and Vigignolles, 1999; Comeau, 1996). By encouraging welfare recipients to work in the not-for-profit sector, the government avoids criticisms that it is providing "cheap labor" for business enterprises. And, by requiring welfare recipients to work on projects aimed at benefiting the community as a whole, the CITs can be presented as being simultaneously "tough on welfare recipients" and "good for society." They thus appeal to a broader range of stakeholder groups and policy publics than more traditional welfare-to-work initiatives.

The ongoing need for compromise among competing advocacy coalitions was well illustrated by the composition of an important committee set up in the mid-1990s to overhaul Quebec's welfare system, the Comité Fortin-Bouchard (Lessard, 1996). Pierre Fortin (an economist) and Camille Bouchard (a psychologist) were generally perceived as spokesmen for the two opposing advocacy coalitions described above.

## The Dynamics of Policy Learning: Assimilation, Accommodation, and "Reconstitution"

Finding policy concepts that are both innovative and value relevant is an important challenge for policy entrepreneurs. New policies must be found that are both "different" and useful, responding to recognized needs in a new and better way. Policy innovation is a symbolic and linguistic process as well as a technical and administrative one. Innovations must build on the structures of meaning already present in society. They are analogous to the reconstitution of existing knowledge during the development of motor skills in young children. As Bourret and Huard describe it (1990, pp. 70–71, author's translation):

> "Accommodation" . . . is a marginal modification of an existing procedure in order to develop a new application. The child learns to grasp a moving object, for example. These two processes—reciprocal accommodation and the establishment of a new equilibrium—are powerful instruments for the development of new abilities.

For Bourret and Huard, this is "endogamous learning." While influenced by external examples, it occurs primarily within the individual "memory system" (Cohen and Levinthal, 1990). The innovative capacity of the memory system, however, also depends on its relations with the external environment (Bourret and Huard, 1990, pp. 74–75):

> Although it is in the productive unit that learning occurs, innovation depends on a particular combination of skills and resources coming from outside. . . . The innovative capacity of an organization depends on its ability to combine openness toward the environment . . . with the maintenance of its internal coherence.

The same point is made by Cohen and Levinthal (1990, p. 133):

> With regard to the absorptive capacity of the firm as a whole, there may . . . be a trade-off in the efficiency of internal communication against the ability of the subunit to assimilate and exploit information originating from other subunits or the environment. This can be seen as a trade-off between inward-looking versus outward-looking absorptive capacities. While both of these

components are necessary for effective organizational learning, excessive dominance by one or the other will be dysfunctional. If all actors in the organization share the same specialized language, they will be effective in communicating with one another, but they may not be able to tap into diverse external knowledge sources.

These examples also illustrate one of the basic premises of the "structural" approach to linguistic analysis (de Saussure, 1974): that terms and concepts derive their meanings not only from the objects they refer to—the things they "stand for"—but also from the whole range of objects that they do not refer to. Social economy, for example, opposes or "excludes" not only the private business economy but also the concept of government control. By the same logic, policies may be valued because they favor particular groups in society or because they penalize certain groups (Ingram and Schneider, 1991).

The CITs are valued in a "substantive" way by certain groups, for example, because they provide services to the elderly—a valued group in Quebec society. But they are also "symbolically" valued by other groups because they impose penalties on welfare recipients, still perceived by many as "welfare bums."

Welfare-to-work programs are known in Quebec and in France as "mesures de réinsertion," rather than as "programmes de transition de l'aide sociale à l'emploi." They are supposed not only to help welfare recipients find work but also to "reintegrate" them into society. Such programs are presented as being part of the *lutte à l'exclusion* (the war against exclusion). The idea is to help groups that are poor and marginalized enjoy the benefits of full participation in society.

However, the struggle against exclusion is not only about poverty. Immigrants can also be excluded, not only because they are poor and unemployed, but also because they are culturally and linguistically distinct from the majority. Partisans of "inclusion" are often critical of the middle-class majority, which "lacks solidarity" with the excluded groups. The welfare ministries in both Quebec and in France are thus called Ministries of Solidarity. Inclusion is thus portrayed as a desired and valued goal of public policy (Aubry and Charest, 1995).

*Inclusion* is a useful concept for the legitimation of welfare-to-work initiatives, as it carries with it values that are clearly established in French society and history. While relatively new as a tool of policy analysis, it appeals to norms whose legitimacy was established long ago, in the decades immediately following the French Revolution.

These ideas—of equality, secularism, and centralization—were particularly important in the views of the Jacobins who dominated French society after the revolution—in contrast to the Girondins who favored decentralization and local diversity. In their successful war for supremacy, the Jacobins portrayed the Girondins as defenders of the old regime. In

France today the notions of decentralization and regional diversity still carry with them connotations of inequality and local privilege. All French citizens in every part of the country, according to the Jacobin ideal, should have exactly the same rights, duties, and privileges as every other French citizen.

While Quebec does not have the same Jacobin values as France, the notions of exclusion and inclusion do resonate within Quebec society and culture, partly because of the francophone majority's struggle to defend its French cultural identity within English-speaking North America. Inclusion in Quebec can thus mean inclusion within the community of Quebec francophones, while exclusion can mean that marginalized groups risk being lost to the francophone majority.

The legitimacy of the CITs, in this perspective, can also be seen as resulting from the fact that they were relevant to two distinct policy communities: the "welfare reform" policy community and the "home care for the elderly" policy community. This was the first time that members of the two policy communities had sought to exploit their mutual "synergies."

If the CITs had been required to finance themselves entirely by the revenues they earned from the private sector, they would probably not have been viable. What made them possible was their ability to provide solutions—or apparent solutions—to the problems faced by both policy communities.

This "coupling" increased home care for the elderly by making possible the employment of the welfare recipients working in the CITs for the provision of home care for the elderly. Since the salaries of CIT employees were subsidized by the Ministry of Employment and Solidarity, the CITs could offer less costly services than those offered by competing agencies.

In this way, it was useful to portray the Corporations intermédiaires du travail as a response to the "failures" of existing welfare-to-work programs. While similar in some respects to the "workfare" orientation adopted in many U.S. states and Canadian provinces, this "made in Quebec" policy innovation sought to capture some of the benefits of workfare while avoiding its more negative connotations. It thus mobilized a broader range of support within Quebec than would be possible with a more explicit workfare orientation.

## Improved "Policy Language" as a Tool of Welfare Reform: The Quebec Case

Evaluation in Quebec has been successful in identifying many of the major obstacles to the effectiveness of existing welfare-to-work programs. Unfortunately—with a few notable exceptions such as the CITs—these evaluations have not been successful in promoting an ongoing process of policy learning.

Perhaps the most important defect of the existing programs, as pointed out by Sylvestre (1994), is that they fail to distinguish between different kinds of welfare recipients. The existing welfare-to-work programs provide approximately the same services to all welfare recipients. As a result, too many welfare recipients receive too few services, while others receive too many.

The "chronic" or long-term welfare recipients who require intensive training, counseling, and follow-up to get off welfare are not provided with the intensive services they require, while short-term welfare recipients who might find a job without training are nevertheless forced to undergo training. Hence the finding (Hamel, Lanctôt, and Sylvestre, 1993) that short-term welfare recipients who do not participate in training assignments are actually more likely to find work than those who do.

By the perverse logic of "performance measurement" that still prevails in Quebec's welfare-to-work programs, many of those who undergo training are precisely those who need it least. Since they are likely to find a job in any case, they are forced to undergo retraining, as a way of "improving the statistics." The fact that they find a job after their training makes it seem that the training helped them find a job—just the opposite, in other words, of what actually happened.

Even if it were possible to find work assignments for every person on welfare—which would be impossible in Quebec—the evidence of earlier program evaluations suggests that universal work assignments would greatly increase the costs and complexity of the welfare system, while actually reducing the proportion of welfare recipients who find permanent employment. People cannot be out looking for work at the same time as they are carrying out compulsory work assignments.

The inability to improve welfare-to-work programs in Quebec is thus not the result of insufficient program evaluation. The problem lies in bringing evaluation results to bear on policy making. This depends on an even more fundamental task, that of "getting the message out." In other words, program evaluators must act as policy entrepreneurs, getting public opinion to understand that there are many different kinds of welfare recipients, and that the measures that are effective and appropriate with one kind of welfare recipient may be quite ineffective and quite inappropriate in dealing with others.

From the "rational" point of view, the necessary reforms are obvious: training resources should be concentrated on those most likely to benefit from them, while those who do not need them should be exempted from them. From a political point of view, however, such a reform is difficult. It is more profitable, politically speaking, to design programs that reflect popular prejudices about welfare recipients and that require all welfare recipients to work "in return for" their welfare payments. This is less expensive than attempts to change the popular misconceptions that constitute an important obstacle to effective welfare reform.

The originality of Quebec's CITs, from this point of view, lay in their founders' recognition that improving welfare-to-work programs cannot be divorced from building popular support for those improvements. By developing a new kind of welfare-to-work program, based on the notions of "inclusion" and "social economy," the promoters of the CITs successfully communicated two important messages. First, that the supply of good work assignments for training welfare recipients is limited. And second, that many welfare recipients will emerge from the welfare system even if they are not forced to undergo government-financed retraining.

The current challenge for program evaluation, in this field and in others, is thus to find ways of communicating to public opinion—and to those groups that are influential in forming public opinion—what is already known by program evaluators. While the CITs provide an interesting example of "spontaneous policy learning," such initiatives are still the exception rather than the rule.

## References

Aubry, F., and Charest, J. *Développer l'économie solidaire. Elements d'orientation.* Montréal: Confédération des syndicats nationaux, Service de recherche, 1995.

Barreto, B., and Vigignolles, Y. *Panorama de l'économie sociale française.* http://www.globenet.org/horizon-local/perso/ecosocfr.html. 1999.

Bellemare, P. "Québec donne-t-il trop aux assistés sociaux?" *La Presse,* Nov. 17, 1995, p. A5.

Boivin, L. "Le sentier boueux de l'économie sociale." *L'Artère,* 1995, *16,* 16–18.

Boivin, L. "L'Économie sociale, ou comment faire passer en douceur la réduction des dépenses sociales de l'Etat." *Temps Fou,* Dec. 1995/Jan. 1996, No. 8–9, pp. 10–11.

Bordeleau, D. "Entre l'exclusion et l'insertion: les entreprises d'insertion au Québec." *Economie et Solidarités,* 1996, *28* (2), 75–94.

Bourret, P., and Huard, P. "Création, appropriation, recomposition: processus innovants dans la production du diagnostic prénatal." *Sciences Sociales et Santé,* 1990, *8,* 4.

Cabatoff, K. "Getting On and Off the Policy Agenda: A Dualistic Theory of Program Evaluation Utilization." *Canadian Journal of Program Evaluation,* 1996, *11,* 2.

Chen, H.-T. *Theory-Driven Evaluation.* Thousand Oaks, Calif.: Sage, 1990.

Cohen, M. D., March, J. G., and Olsen, J. P. "A Garbage Can Model of Organizational Choice." *Administrative Science Quarterly,* 1972, *17,* 1–25.

Cohen, W. M., and Levinthal, D. A. "Absorptive Capacity: A New Perspective on Learning and Innovation." *Administrative Science Quarterly,* 1990, *35,* 128–152.

Comeau, Y. "Problématique de l'exclusion et approches d'insertion." *Economie et Solidarités,* 1996, *28* (2), 11–22.

Cronbach, L. J., and Associates. *Toward Reform of Program Evaluation.* San Francisco: Jossey-Bass, 1980.

Cyert, R. M., Simon, H. A., and Trow, D. B. "Observation of a Business Decision." In G. A. Yukl and K. N. Wexley (eds.), *Readings in Organizational and Industrial Psychology.* New York: Oxford University Press, 1971, pp. 107–118.

Defourny, J., and Monzon Campos, J. L. (eds). *Economie sociale: entre Économie capitaliste et économie publique.* (The third sector: cooperative, mutual, and nonprofit organizations.) Brussels: CIRIEC, De Boeck Université, 1992, pp. 385–446.

de Saussure, F. *Course in General Linguistics.* Glasgow, Scotland: Fontana, 1974.

Gouvernement du Québec. *Les corporations intermédiaires de travail, Formule pour faciliter l'insertion des personnes sans emploi.* Québec: Ministère de la Main-d'oeuvre, de la Sécurité du revenu et de la Formation professionnelle, 1993a.

Gouvernement du Québec. *Note explicative: Les corporations intermédiaires de travail.* Québec: Direction de la main-d'oeuvre et de l'intégration à l'emploi, Ministère de la Main-d'oeuvre, de la Sécurité du revenu et de la Formation professionnelle, 1993b.

Hamel, S., Lanctôt, P., and Sylvestre, C. *Les effets non désirés relatifs à la participation aux mesures, analyse quantitative.* Québec: Ministère de la Main-d'Oeuvre, de la Sécurité du revenu et de la Formation professionnelle, 1993.

Ingram, H., and Schneider, A. "The Choice of Target Populations." *Administration and Society,* 1991, *23* (3), 333–356.

Kingdon, J. W. *Agendas, Alternatives, and Public Policies.* Boston: Little, Brown, 1984.

Lessard, D. "Le travail des 'boubou-macoutes' a donné de bien maigres résultats." *La Presse,* Nov. 6, 1993, p. A1.

Lessard, D. "Vers une 'allocation familiale unifiée'. Le comité Fortin-Bouchard proposera des pistes pour inciter les assistés sociaux à retourner sur le marché du travail." *La Presse,* Feb. 13, 1996, p. B1.

March, J. G., and Olsen, J. P. *Ambiguity and Choice in Organizations.* Bergen, Norway: Universitetsforlaget, 1976.

Normand, G. "Tous les assistés sociaux aptes au travail seront rencontrés." *La Presse,* Feb. 17, 1996, p. A20.

Patton, M. Q. *Utilization-Focused Evaluation.* Thousand Oaks, Calif.: Sage, 1986.

Patton, M. Q. "The Evaluator's Responsibility for Utilization." *Evaluation Practice,* 1988, *9* (2), 5–24.

Sabatier, P. A. "An Advocacy Coalition Framework of Policy Change and the Role of Policy-Oriented Learning Therein." *Policy Sciences,* 1988, *21,* 129–168.

Sabatier, P. A., and Jenkins-Smith, H. C. (eds.). *Policy Change and Learning: An Advocacy Coalition Approach.* Boulder, Colo.: Westview Press, 1993.

Sylvestre, C. *Synthèse des résultats des études d'évaluation en matière de développement de l'employabilité et d'intégration en emploi.* Québec: Ministère de la Sécurité du revenu, 1994.

*Kenneth Cabatoff is associate professor of political science at the Université du Québec à Montréal. From 1997 to 1999 he was president of the Quebec Program Evaluation Society.*

5

*The language used in mixed-sex focus groups and the resulting potential for missing information are discussed in this chapter.*

# Sociolinguistic Dynamics of Gender in Focus Groups

*Courtney L. Brown*

The relationship between gender and language has been a part of research studies since the beginning of the twentieth century, starting with the work of Otto Jespersen (1922). The work of Robin Lakoff (1975) brought gender and language to the forefront of linguistic research, and it has remained there for the past quarter century. It is now a sociolinguistic fact that men and women differ in their communicative behavior (Coates, 1989; Gal, 1994). Research has found men's speaking styles to be more dominant in mixed-sex conversations (Swann, 1989; Tannen, 1994; Zimmerman and West, 1975). Men speak longer (Woods, 1989), speak more about themselves (Tannen, 1990), interrupt more (Woods, 1989), use fewer politeness strategies (Coates, 1993), take on more of a leadership position (Carli, 1989), and use fewer verbal and nonverbal signs of attentiveness in conversation (LaFrance, 1981; Tannen, 1994) than do women. Research has shown that these male strategies silence women (Coates, 1993; Zimmerman and West, 1975). If we accept these studies as true, problems may arise in evaluations that use mixed-sex focus groups.

Focus groups have become an important and common form of research in the social sciences (Stewart and Shamdasani, 1990). Focus groups are beneficial because they produce a type of data that other methods do not. They provide a "rich and detailed set of data about perceptions, thoughts, feelings, and impressions of group members in members' own words" (Stewart and Shamdasani, 1990, p. 140). They allow the participants to be the experts of their own lives and social worlds. Focus groups are grounded in the "human tendency to discuss issues and ideas in groups" (Sink, 1991, p. 197). A good focus group creates a social environment in which group members are stimulated by the perceptions and ideas of each other. It is a forum for full participation and interaction and offers evaluators more depth of data than would be gathered from individual interviews.

## Language in Focus Groups

When gender-driven language differences are combined in a group setting, dynamics occur that may hinder the focus group purpose and thus the evaluation process. Many focus group experts recommend using homogeneous groups based on the reason for the research or evaluation (Frey and Fontana, 1993; Krueger, 1994; Vaughn, Schumm, and Sinagub, 1996), and in many cases this means separating the sexes (Goldman and McDonald, 1987; Stewart and Shamdasani, 1990). Stewart and Shamdasani (1990) claim that the "nature of the interaction and the quality of the data obtained from focus groups will be influenced by the gender composition of the group" (p. 43). Many focus groups, except those specifically directed at one sex or the other (such as focus groups on feminine products or men's views on prostate cancer) do mix the sexes, and when they do, they do not take the quality and reliability of the data into account during analysis.

The language participants use and/or do not use in focus groups is vital to how evaluators analyze data. If focus groups are to continue as a prevalent research tool, studies on their methodology must be conducted. In David Morgan's book, *Successful Focus Groups: Advancing the State of the Art* (1993), he writes that more research must be conducted on the homogeneity and heterogeneity of groups and how they affect what participants are willing to say. An understanding of gender dynamics is crucial. The accuracy standard in the second edition of *The Program Evaluation Standards* (Joint Committee on Standards for Education Evaluation, 1994) ensures that a good evaluation will state and convey technically adequate information, which includes valid and reliable measures. If women are silenced in mixed-sex focus groups, the reliability and the quality of the data come into question. This chapter examines language differences between men and women and the dynamics that occur when they are brought together in a focus group. This is illustrated through a series of eleven mixed-sex focus groups. A discussion of the concerns and dangers of these language dynamics regarding evaluation follows and concludes with recommendations for future mixed-sex focus groups.

## The Language in Evaluation as Seen in Mixed-Sex Focus Groups

This study sought to examine whether men and women participate equally in evaluations using mixed-sex focus groups. In order to determine this, eleven archived focus group transcripts were examined. These transcripts came from focus group studies run at two different East Coast living history museums in 1995 and 1996. The focus groups were not run for the purposes of this study, but were conducted as evaluations for the museums. Afterward, the museums gave this researcher permission to use the focus group transcripts and videotapes for purposes of this present study.

The audiotapes, videotapes, and transcripts of the eleven focus groups were examined using both quantitative and qualitative methodology. Quantitative methods were employed only to obtain a count of how much each participant spoke. This was done with a simple count of the number of lines in a transcript. The major thrust of this study was qualitative. The codes and categories used were both predetermined and emergent. The predetermined codes were based in the literature review of current theories and findings in sociolinguistics (Maxwell, 1996). The emergent categories were based on recurring themes found in the data (Lincoln and Guba, 1985; Maxwell, 1996).

A basic case study was written on each of the focus groups. These cases were then divided into two groups, those focus groups with more women and those focus groups with more men. Afterward a cross-case analysis was conducted on each group. Finally a cross-case analysis of all eleven focus groups was written. This analysis looked at the issues across all cases and assisted in supporting an overall explanation and theory for gender dynamics in mixed-sex focus groups.

## Results from the Cross-Case Analysis of All Focus Groups

A variety of overriding themes emerged from each case. The predetermined and emergent codes used were body language, talking time, floor-taking strategies, topic raising, and leadership emergence. These are each discussed in detail below.

**Body Language.**   The first of the broad themes is body language. Body language refers to body positioning and the use of nonverbal signals to convey meaning. This theme includes what the majority of the participants were found to do. It does not include the frequent female speaker or the leader. These will be discussed in detail under the leadership emergence theme. In examination of the videotapes, the body positioning of the participants was the most obvious and striking difference between men and women. They tended to sit in opposite positions. The women usually sat close to the table while the men leaned back from the table. This was consistent with the literature, which states that men and women often take on such positions in conversation (Coates, 1993). When another participant had the floor and was speaking, the women tended to look at that person and often smiled and nodded. However, when a female had the floor she often did not look at the other participants. She usually looked at the moderator or down at the table. The men, on the other hand, tended to exhibit exactly the opposite behavior. When another participant had the floor the men generally looked down at the table or at their hands. When a man took the floor either by interruption or by being called on, he usually looked up and addressed the entire group by looking at each one of the participants. Women's use of smiles and nods was also found by Davis and Weitz (1981); however, their use of eye contact was only half-consistent with what Coates (1993) found. She found that women tend to look at other participants throughout conversations while men typically avoid looking at others. In this study women tended to make eye contact while others were speaking whereas men characteristically looked at other participants only when they themselves were speaking.

This study's findings may be different from what Coates found because while she looked at conversation, this study examined focus groups. Focus groups are a unique communicative event because a moderator is employed to ask questions and maintain the flow of conversation. For these reasons the moderator is in a position of power. This power seems to have been acknowledged by the women because they signaled their desire to speak to her and directed their question responses to her. The men did not overtly acknowledge the moderator's power. This may have been due to the fact that the moderator in all focus groups was a woman.

**Talking Time.** Many researchers claim that talking time is a sign of power. Bales (1973) stated that the more a speaker speaks the more power he or she has. For use in this case, talking time was measured quantitatively by the number of transcript lines. A line consists of any verbal response made by a participant. This could be as short as a "Yes" or long enough to fill the entire line. In order to examine all of the focus groups together, all of the data were compiled and are shown in Table 5.1 as the total talking time across all cases of male talk time versus female talk time.

Table 5.1 demonstrates a number of things about talking time of men and women in the eleven focus groups. It is important to notice first that there are two types of talk, structured and unstructured. This is because the focus groups were conducted in two parts. The first part of every question was structured. Structured meant that the moderator went around the table and directly asked every participant the same question. After each person

**Table 5.1. Percentage of Male versus Female Talking Time in Mixed-Sex Focus Groups**

| | | | Types of Talk | | Types of Unstructured Talk | | |
|---|---|---|---|---|---|---|---|
| Sex | # | % | Structured | Unstructured | Minimal Response | Called On | Not Called On |
| M | 54 | 56% | 56% | 60% | 1% | 8% | 91% |
| F | 43 | 44% | 44% | 40% | 16% | 64% | 20% |

had responded, the floor was open to anyone to build on what someone else had said, to refute what someone else had said, or to raise a new idea. This was considered the unstructured part. Men made up 56 percent of the participants and they spoke 56 percent of the time in the structured portion. Women made up about 44 percent of the participants and they spoke 44 percent of the structured portion. This confirms Sommers and Lawrence (cited in Tannen, 1994) who found that when handed the floor in turn, as was done in the structured portion of each focus group, men and women speak equally. In the unstructured portion of the focus groups, however, the women spoke less. The women spoke only 40 percent of the time while the men spoke 60 percent. Even though the women decreased their speaking time in the unstructured portion, it was by only 4 percent. Quantitatively this seems to be a very small percentage and not enough to say that men spoke more. This refutes what many researchers have found. In Krueger's (1994) research on focus groups, he found that men have a tendency to speak more in mixed-sex groups. Aries (1976) also found that men took up the most time in mixed-sex interactions. In the present study, however, men and women, given their unequal numbers, spoke in proportionate amounts.

This finding may also have been a result of the very nature of focus groups and more specifically the focus groups used in this study. First of all, focus groups employ a moderator. A moderator maintains the flow of the discussion and encourages every participant to speak. Normal conversations do not have a moderator and thus no one to ensure participation of all members of the conversation. Secondly, these focus groups were conducted in two parts, as mentioned previously: they had a structured and an unstructured part. In normal conversations and in most focus groups, this speaking opportunity and direct questioning, as in the structured part, is not offered to every participant in turn. Finally, these findings may be different from the literature because of the quantitative coding device used. This device counted participant speaking amounts by the number of lines each had in the transcript. Every line was counted as one regardless of whether it had twenty words or only one. Since the women provided the majority of minimal responses and supportive one-word lines, such as "yeah" and "uh-huh," their quantitative contribution is actually inflated in the tables. Therefore, it can be speculated that the findings in this study differed from those in the literature due to three factors: the fact that a focus group is a unique communicative event unlike conversations and group discussions; the methods used in the focus groups examined for this study; and the quantitative coding device.

However, to determine who contributed more content, this study went beyond a quantitative examination of the number of spoken lines in a transcript and looked at the qualitative aspect of what was said. The following sections analyze how much was spoken by each sex in the focus groups.

**Floor-Taking Strategies.** Men and women used very different strategies to take the floor in the focus groups. Table 5.1 shows that of women's unstructured contributions, 64 percent were initiated because the moderator called on them. Women most often were called to speak after using a nonverbal signals, such as raised eyebrows or a raised finger, to convey their desire to speak. Afterward they patiently waited until they were called on before beginning to speak. Once they were called on they frequently introduced their speech with a verbal expression of a desire to speak:

> Lisa: I would like to say something about that too.

The women also regularly introduced their new remarks by building on what the previous person had said.

> Angela: Uh, mine is along the same line as his (Warren) uh, having people there be in the time, umm, acting it out. (She spent nine more lines of text repeating Warren's point before she got to her own which took only two lines.) Something on paper where you can look and just a short, quick little definition that you can relay the information off of.

This confirms Brown and Levinson's (1987) study on politeness, which says that women often request to speak and introduce new remarks by building on what previous people have said in order to be polite. Since men in this study did not use these same politeness strategies, it thus helps to support Reeder's (1995) assertions that women are more polite than men are.

Although the women frequently made nonverbal requests to speak, men did not offer them the floor. Instead the moderator had to call on them to speak. Maccoby (cited in Tannen, 1994) found similarities in her studies. She discovered that women often wait for a turn that men rarely offer. When women took the floor without being called on, which was only 20 percent of the women's use of the unstructured time, it was most often after a woman had finished speaking (61 percent) or the moderator had asked a question (29 percent). Only 10 percent of the women's time speaking up without being called on was spent speaking up directly after a man had given up the floor. The women did not use any interruptions with men, another woman, or the moderator.

Women in all eleven cases frequently dropped the volume at the end of their turns and as a result the last word or words they spoke became almost inaudible. This gave the women an unconfident quality. Brown and Levinson (1987) found that women often weaken their statement so as not to commit a face-threatening act. Therefore, this may not have been a lack of confidence, but simply a politeness strategy used by women to decrease the strength of their messages, make them more indirect, and protect face of the other participants.

Many studies (Eckert and McConnell-Ginet, 1994; Swann, 1989; Zimmerman and West, 1975; Woods, 1989) have found that men are interrupters. This present study corroborates the literature. It was found that men most often, 91 percent of the unstructured time, took the floor without being called on or using nonverbal signals. The majority of this was in the form of interruptions. When the majority of the men desired to speak they usually took the floor immediately without waiting for the current speaker to finish his or her turn. They also spoke up regardless of whether a male or female currently held the floor or had just given up the floor.

**Topic Raising.** When women and men were offered the floor in turn as they were in the structured portion, they offered thorough and insightful comments. However, only the topics raised by men were developed and built on by the other participants. While the men raised the topics the women supported them:

> Shirlynn: Umm, I was impressed with that too. (Refers to Bill)
>
> Jeannie: Like he (Peter) had mentioned earlier, there was just a couple of trailers.
>
> Betty: Yes, I kinda go along the same line as him. (Looking at Jim)

This same finding was discovered by Swann (1989) who determined that the topics of men are more often pursued while women support their topics. Carli (1989) found similar results in her research that showed women display greater agreement and take on others' topics more often than raising topics themselves.

The topics that women did raise were usually greeted with a nonresponse and were ignored by the other participants. In a few instances these topics were later successfully reintroduced by one of the men who claimed the topic as his own. The other focus group participants then gave the man credit for the topic instead of the woman who originally raised it. In a study of focus groups, Tannen (1994) had similar findings. In her study she sat in on focus groups. Afterward she assumed a man had been responsible for the topics because he had spoken about them in depth and had been given credit for raising the issues. However, after careful examination of the transcripts she found that a woman had actually originally raised the topics for which the man had received credit.

**Leadership Emergence.** The literature mentions several factors that determine power in a group setting. Diamond (1996) mentions three characteristics that determine power: acquisition and retention of the floor, successful topic raising, and interruption. Lakoff (1975) asserts that nonresponse is used by the powerful against the powerless. Bales (1973) claims that power comes from a greater talking time. In accordance with this literature, men were found to have greater power than women in these focus groups under study. Men's topics were successfully raised while women waited to be called on and never used interruptions. Nonresponse was a tool used by men against women, never the other way around. The one area where this study did not agree with the literature was the amount of talking time. The men did not spend a significantly larger amount of time talking than the women. Therefore, talk time did not indicate power in this study. It can be speculated that this may also have been a result of the particular focus groups under study. The focus groups in this study were organized so that each participant was given equal opportunity to respond to each question. This may have resulted in relatively equal speaking time for both men and women.

A man was determined the leader in all eleven focus groups. This was based on the eye contact and responses of the other participants toward this person, successful topic raising, a confident manner, and eye contact of the leader toward the other participants while he spoke. These four characteristics verify what was found in the literature. In addition it corroborates Cragan and Wright (1995) who say the leader is the person everyone looks at. In this study everyone, men and women, looked at the leader when he spoke and often nodded or offered minimal responses. Talking time did not play a role in leadership. As Diamond (1996) found, the quality of what the person was saying as perceived by others was more important for leadership than the quantity of how much he or she spoke.

None of the women fit all four characteristics of leadership, but some women did play an important role in the focus groups. These women were termed Frequent Female Speakers (FFS). This name is fitting because these women spoke a high percentage of time in the structured portion, unstructured portion, or both. Out of the forty-three women in the eleven focus groups, only six women fit into the category of FFS. These women not only spoke a great deal, but also displayed certain masculine attributes. When an FFS spoke she addressed and looked at every participant just as the males did. The FFSes spoke confidently and only rarely dropped their volume at the end of a turn. Most important, the FFSes did not seem intimidated by the men and seemed very comfortable speaking. Carli (1989) found that when they're attempting to be influential, both men and women show a decrease in stereotypically feminine behavior and an increase in masculine behavior. The FFSes did incorporate some masculine behavior, but also maintained some feminine characteristics. They nodded and smiled at other speakers and they supported the topics introduced by others. Regardless of these masculine and feminine demeanors, the male participants essentially ignored the FFSes. Although these women contributed a great deal to their focus groups, the males did not acknowledge their contributions and none of the FFSes emerged as leader.

Just as the prominent women from the focus groups exhibited some male characteristics, some of the male leaders exhibited some female characteristics. Many of the leaders sat up to the table throughout the session as the women did. Some also looked at other speakers and nodded as the women did instead of looking down when someone else had the floor as the majority of the men did. Kent and Moss (1994) discovered that sex had no effect on leader emergence, but gender role did. Regardless of the sex, masculine subjects were more likely to emerge as leaders than females. This study found that masculine behavior and language are important to leadership emergence, but it also discovered that some female behavior, such as sitting up to the table and looking at other speakers, also play a role in leadership characteristics.

## Findings

The analysis of the data and emergent themes indicates that the conversational styles employed by men create an imbalance of participation. The overriding themes that emerged from the data show that men and women used language in quite different ways to take the floor. Men were very assertive: when they desired the floor they often took it through interruption. Men regularly used verbal means for taking the floor, which simply meant that they began to speak and state their fact or opinion. Women, on the contrary, typically used nonverbal means of obtaining the floor. They made signals—raising a hand, raising eyebrows, and so on—as a means of conveying a desire to speak. Afterward they patiently waited for the moderator to call on them to speak.

Women used nonverbal and verbal strategies to present support to other participants in a polite manner. They smiled and nodded while others spoke. They used minimal responses to provide encouragement and understanding. When women desired to speak they seldom did so without being asked to speak by the moderator. Once women had the floor they supported topics introduced by others instead of introducing their own topics.

The verbal strategies used by men were assertive. They frequently interrupted both men and women. When a man was interrupted he took the floor back by using an interruption himself; however, when a woman was interrupted she remained silent until the moderator called on her. Men also silenced women by ignoring their ideas and topics. Men only very rarely supported the topics raised by women. In fact when a woman did raise a new topic it was either completely ignored by the group or reintroduced by a man and instead of giving her credit for it he claimed it as his own. As a result, conversational styles used by men were found to silence women in this study.

From a strictly quantitative viewpoint men's and women's voices were heard equally. However, from a qualitative viewpoint there was a great difference. Instead of providing new topics, women spent a greater amount of time playing a supportive role. They used minimal responses and built on topics introduced by men. The men, on the other hand, supplied more of the content of the focus groups. They introduced new topics, opinions, and ideas. Therefore, in this study, men participated more in the focus group and provided more concrete data to the focus group study.

It was originally believed that the sex composition of the focus group would influence the roles and participation within those groups. It was for this reason that the focus groups were divided into those with more women and those with more men. After careful analysis of the data it was found that this was not the case at all. In the focus group with only one man and five women the man's behavior was no different from the men's behavior in focus groups with a majority of men. The only time sex composition seemed to influence gender roles was in the focus group with only one woman and eight men. In this case the woman began to mimic the body positioning of the men; she leaned back in her chair as they did. However, none of her other feminine behaviors changed. In the other cases a majority either way did not influence or alter the language use or behaviors of either sex.

## Dangers of Ignoring Gender Language Differences in Evaluation

Guideline A under the Human Interactions Standard (P4) of *The Program Evaluation Standards* (Joint Committee on Standards for Education Evaluation, 1994) says, "Make every effort to understand the culture, social values, and language differences of the participants" (p. 99). Recognizing and understanding that language differences exist between the sexes is crucial to the reliability and validity of a good evaluation. It will also help reduce the potential bias that could occur when women are silenced and only men's ideas are heard. This study has demonstrated that men and women employ different language strategies in mixed-group settings. Although women and men quantitatively spoke almost equal amounts in both the structured and unstructured portions, they did not equally contribute to the focus groups. The men almost always spoke about the object of the focus group: the museums. They introduced new topics and ideas and sometimes built on other men's topics. The women, on the other hand, spent relatively more time in both the structured and the unstructured portions offering minimal responses and building on men's topics. They frequently played a supportive role in the focus groups while men played a content role. The gender and language dynamics in these focus groups tended to silence women.

The strength of the focus group methodology is the conversational exchange that occurs among all involved. In good focus groups participants build on one another's ideas and help to construct a greater and deeper understanding of the topic. However, if this does not happen because women are silenced, the data may be unreliable and low in quality. This can be dangerous to evaluations that rely on focus groups as a method of data collection.

Many believe a well-trained moderator can circumvent these problems and ensure equal involvement of participants. However, a moderator can only make sure everyone participates. A moderator cannot make participants offer rich feelings and thoughts, introduce new ideas, disagree with others' ideas, or speak for equally long periods of time. A moderator can only keep the conversation flowing, encourage those who are silent, and discourage those who are dominant.

## Recommendations

The following recommendations are based on the findings of this study. The use of these recommendations will depend on the purpose and the topic of the evaluation and focus group. Without further research, only a few cautious recommendations can be made:

- Prior to the beginning of the focus group, discuss clear "rules of discourse." These would include: encouraging all participants to offer opinions, informing participants they do not need to receive permission prior to speaking, encouraging all to be respectful of the others, and explaining that participants should address their comments to the group, not the moderator. These "rules" should keep the conversation flowing, encourage new opinions from all, and limit the number of interruptions.
- Employ aggressive moderators. The moderators should work to ensure that women are not silenced. This can be accomplished if the moderators are extremely observant and responsive to the nonverbal signals of women. They must also encourage those who are silent and discourage those who are dominant.
- Do not use mixed-sex focus groups. If the evaluation budget is sufficient and the topic is amenable, separate focus groups could be conducted with men and women.
- Do not do anything. If the goal of the focus group is to mirror social interactions of how women and men interact in mixed-sex groups, then nothing should be done. If this is how men and women really interact, and a key purpose of the focus group is to gather "real life" data, then there is no problem. However, if the goal is to gain new and deeper insights into the topic from all participants, something must be done.

One must be cautious not to overgeneralize the results from this study. The participants, while randomly chosen to participate in the museum's focus groups, came from a very homogenous population. The majority was white, upper-middle-class, and well educated. They came from all over the country, but most were in the area on family vacations. The focus groups were conducted in two parts, a structured portion and an unstructured portion. Most focus groups do not employ this method but instead have a more open-ended unstructured forum. When examining this study one must do so through the above lenses. Regardless, one can see the potential dangers of these gender-based language dynamics to evaluations that use focus groups as a data collection method. It is the recommendation of this researcher that caution be taken when conducting and interpreting data from focus groups for evaluations.

## References

Aries, E. "Interaction Patterns and Themes of Male, Female, and Mixed Groups." *Small Group Behavior*, 1976, 7, 7–18.

Bales, R. F. "Communication in Small Groups." In G. Miller (ed.), *Communication, Language and Meaning: Psychological Perspectives*. New York: Basic Books, 1973.

Brown, P., and Levinson, S. *Politeness: Some Universals in Language Use.* New York: Cambridge University Press, 1987.

Carli, L. L. "Gender Differences in Interaction Style." *Journal of Personality and Social Psychology,* 1989, *56,* 565–576.

Coates, J. Introduction in J. Coates and D. Cameron (eds.), *Women in Their Speech Communities.* New York: Longman, 1989.

Coates, J. *Women, Men, and Language.* New York: Longman, 1993.

Cragan, J. F., and Wright, D. W. *Communication in Small Groups: Theory, Process, Skills.* (4th ed.) St. Paul, Minn.: West Publishing, 1995.

Davis, M., and Weitz, S. "Sex Differences in Body Movements and Positions." In C. Mayo and N. Henley (eds.), *Gender and Nonverbal Behavior.* New York: Springer-Veriag, 1981.

Diamond, J. *Status and Power in Verbal Interaction.* Philadelphia: John Benjamins Publishing, 1996.

Eckert, P., and McConnell-Ginet, S. "Think Practically and Look Locally: Language and Gender as Community Based Practice." In C. Roman, S. Juhasz, and C. Miller (eds.), *The Women and Language Debate: A Sourcebook.* New Brunswick, N.J.: Rutgers University Press, 1994.

Frey, J. H., and Fontana, A. "The Group Interview in Social Research." In D. L. Morgan (ed.), *Successful Focus Groups: Advancing the State of the Art.* Thousand Oaks, Calif.: Sage, 1993.

Gal, S. "Between Speech and Silence: The Problematics of Research on Language and Gender." In C. Roman, S. Juhasz, and C. Miller (eds.), *The Women and Language Debate: A Sourcebook.* New Brunswick, N.J.: Rutgers University Press, 1994.

Goldman, A. E., and McDonald, S. S. *The Group Depth Interview: Principles and Practice.* Upper Saddle River, N.J.: Prentice Hall, 1987.

Jespersen, O. "The Woman." *Language: Its Nature, Development and Origins.* London: Allen Unwin, 1922.

The Joint Committee on Standards for Educational Evaluation. *The Program Evaluation Standards.* (2nd ed.) Thousand Oaks, Calif.: Sage, 1994.

Kent, R., and Moss, S. "Effects on Sex and Gender Role on Leader Emergence." *Academy of Management Journal,* 1994, *37,* 1335–1346.

Krueger, R. A. *Focus Groups: A Practical Guide for Applied Research.* (2nd ed.) Thousand Oaks, Calif.: Sage, 1994.

LaFrance, M. "Gender Gestures: Sex, Sex-Role, and Nonverbal Communication." In C. Mayo and N. Henley (eds.), *Gender and Nonverbal Behavior.* New York: Springer-Veriag, 1981.

Lakoff, R. *Language and Woman's Place.* New York: HarperCollins, 1975.

Lincoln, Y. S., and Guba, E. G. *Naturalistic Inquiry.* Thousand Oaks, Calif.: Sage, 1985.

Maxwell, J. A. *Qualitative Research Design: An Interactive Approach.* Thousand Oaks, Calif.: Sage, 1996.

Morgan, D. L. (ed.). *Successful Focus Groups: Advancing the State of the Art.* Thousand Oaks, Calif.: Sage, 1993.

Reeder, H. M. "Using Focus Groups to Design a Quantitative Measure: Women's Indirect 'No' to Sexual Intimacy." Paper presented at the annual meeting of the Speech Communication Association, San Antonio, Tex., Nov. 1995.

Sink, J. M. "Focus Groups as an Approach to Outcome Assessment." *American Review of Public Administration,* 1991, *21,* 197–204.

Stewart, D. W., and Shamdasani, P. N. *Focus Groups: Theory and Practice.* Thousand Oaks, Calif.: Sage, 1990.

Swann, J. "Talk Control: An Illustration from the Classroom of Problems in Analyzing Male Dominance of Conversation." In J. Coates and D. Cameron (eds.), *Women in Their Speech Communities.* New York: Longman, 1989.

Tannen, D. *Talking From 9 to 5.* New York: William Morrow & Co., 1994.

Tannen, D. *You Just Don't Understand: Women and Men in Conversation.* New York: Ballantine Books, 1990.

Vaughn, S., Schumm, J. S., and Sinagub, J. *Focus Group Interviews in Education and Psychology.* Thousand Oaks, Calif.: Sage, 1996.

Woods, N. "Talking Shop: Sex and Status as Determinants of Floor Apportionment in a Work Setting." In J. Coates and D. Cameron (eds.), *Women in Their Speech Communities.* New York: Longman, 1989.

Zimmerman, D., and West, C. "Sex Roles, Interruptions and Silences in Conversation." In B. Thorne and N. Henley (eds.), *Language and Sex: Difference and Dominance.* Rowley, Mass: Rowley House, 1975.

*COURTNEY L. BROWN is an adjunct professor of educational research and assessment in the department of educational studies at Purdue University. Her major research interests are sociolinguistics and evaluation.*

6

*As our language of evaluation changes, so do the metaphors we use to describe our work. In this chapter, the author discusses how examining metaphors in language of individuals and groups offers insight into how people frame and resolve problems.*

# Beyond the Literal: Metaphors and Why They Matter

*Alexis Kaminsky*

In their book, *Foundations of Program Evaluation*, Shadish, Cook, and Leviton (1991) assert that evaluation theory's purpose is "to specify feasible practices that evaluators can use to construct knowledge of the value of social programs that can be used to ameliorate the social problems to which programs are relevant" (p. 36). This purpose has been interpreted in many ways over evaluation's thirty-plus-year history from conventional readings in which evaluators used their expertise to provide scientific knowledge to decision makers (Campbell's experimenting society, for example) to emancipatory versions in which evaluators actively promote change for the most disenfranchised of society (for example: Mertens, 1999; Whitmore, 1999). As the field's perspectives on what evaluation is and can be have proliferated, so has the language we use to talk about our work.

Multiple sources have contributed to the construction of our language *of* evaluation. Many commonplace concepts have been brought to the field by individuals trained in other areas or disciplines (Cook, 1997; Weiss, 1998). Some of our earliest language for how to do our work—experiments and later quasi-experiments—reflect the evaluators' psychology background (Cook, 1997). Other terms have been borrowed from fields such education, sociology, political theory, and organizational development. Still other language is created specifically for evaluation; the concept *stakeholder* quickly comes to mind. In my experience, the language individual evaluators use—whether brought, borrowed, or created—frames how they think about and practice their work. I believe that our *language of evaluation* as a field shapes a wider evaluation agenda, defining the issues we consider and the solutions that we seek.

NEW DIRECTIONS FOR EVALUATION, no. 86, Summer 2000   © Jossey-Bass

Like Lakoff and Johnson (1980), I believe that "since communication is based on the same conceptual system that we use in thinking and acting, language is an important source of evidence for what that system is like" (p. 3). I suggest here that while language represents how people think and act, metaphor frames these processes. Metaphors can provide insight into the assumptions and values that frame language. As such, metaphors can be powerful means by which evaluators can gain access to how people think and act. In this chapter, I examine how the language *of* evaluation conveys values, intentions, and deeply held assumptions about evaluation practice and its purpose. Specifically, I explore how the "metaphors" we use to talk about evaluation shape what we consider to be important problems and how to resolve them. To illustrate how metaphors work I draw on *language of evaluation* writ large—that is, of the field broadly. I also provide a practical example of looking at metaphors in language from a case study I conducted in the context of higher education. On the basis of these examples, I conclude with some implications, both positive and not-so-positive, for evaluators.

## How Metaphors Work and Their Value for Evaluators

In their book, *Metaphors We Live By*, Lakoff and Johnson (1980) write, "Metaphor is pervasive in everyday life, not just in language but in thought and action" (p. 3). Metaphors are *used consciously* and are *in use* unconsciously. Used consciously, metaphors enrich what our words communicate (Black, 1993). Poets and scientists alike regularly use metaphors in this way. People use metaphors "because we often need to do so, the available literal resources of the language being insufficient to express our sense of the rich correspondences, interrelations, and analogies of domains conventionally separated" (Black, 1993, p. 33). Many evaluators, especially those well practiced in working with qualitative data, know the importance of attending to the metaphors program staff, participants, and other stakeholders use to portray their perspectives and experiences.

*In use* unconsciously, metaphors cue people about what information is most useful to solving problems. These metaphors work as "frames," guiding how individuals first conceptualize, then solve problems (House, 1986; Schon, 1993). Metaphor as frame presents a logic, if you will, for why "certain elements of the situation are included in the story while others are omitted" (Schön, 1993, p. 149).

Different metaphors frame problems using different sets of assumptions about what problems are and how to fix them. Schön (1993) describes how this happens in the language of social policy:

> When we examine the problem-setting told by analysts and practitioners of social policy, it becomes apparent that the *framing of problems often depends upon metaphors underlying the stories which generate problem setting and set the*

*directions of problem solving.* One of the most pervasive stories about social services, for example, diagnoses the problem as "fragmentation" and prescribes "coordination" as the remedy. But services seen as fragmented might be seen, alternatively, as autonomous. . . . Under the spell of metaphor, it appears obvious that fragmentation is bad and coordination, good. . . . This sense of *obviousness depends very much on the metaphor remaining tacit* [p. 138, emphasis added].

In this way, metaphors can be as dangerous as they are valuable to evaluators. As Schön suggests here, metaphors are most influential in restricting the options considered by framing the problem and its parameters in the first place. One challenge as evaluators, then, is how to make influential metaphors explicit.

Before moving on to some examples, let me take a moment to point out a few aspects of metaphor particularly relevant for evaluators. First, as suggested in the paragraphs above, the degree of consciousness that people have about the metaphors they use is important. How aware are we and our stakeholders of the metaphorical frames we use when evaluating social programs and determining their value? Second, metaphors shape the language of individuals as well as the discourse within and between groups. What can we learn by examining how metaphors are used in conversation? By how they are adapted or rejected? Third, for a metaphor to be powerful (to embed itself unconsciously in how people think or to be adopted consciously), it needs to be "generative" (Schön, 1993). It needs to stimulate the imagination to explore unlikely connections and conjure up a wealth of associations. Finally, when analyzing the value of metaphors, evaluators need to remember that metaphors must be understood in the context in which they were used. In the two sections that follow, I illustrate these points about metaphors in the context of our language *of* evaluation as a field as well as in the field through an example from my own practice.

## Metaphors in the Language *of* Evaluation: A Wide-Lens Perspective

Toward the beginning of this chapter, I observed the variety of ways we have acquired a language of evaluation as a field. I suggested that as our vocabulary has changed, so have the metaphors that structure how we think about and practice our work. Much of our language of evaluation reflects all that we have learned. But some of our language, I believe, continues to limit our ability to respond in new ways to perennial challenges to evaluation practice. Let me illustrate with a few metaphors that have framed how evaluators have talked about producing "good" knowledge. I suggest that while still not agreeing about what "good" knowledge is, our differences have stimulated healthy conversation about critical topics.

I'd like to introduce this discussion of good knowledge in evaluation by demonstrating what examining metaphors in our language looks like. I start with a brief analysis of an excerpt from Kuhn's (1970) *Structure of Scientific Revolutions*:

> [O]ne of the things a scientific community acquires with a paradigm is a criterion for choosing problems that, while the paradigm is taken for granted, can be assumed to have solutions. To a great extent these are the only problems that the community will admit as scientific or encourage its members to undertake. Other problems, including many that had previously been standard, are rejected as metaphysical, as the concern of another discipline, or sometimes as just too problematic to be worth the time. A paradigm can, for that matter, even insulate the community from those socially important problems that are not reducible to the puzzle form, because they cannot be stated in terms of the conceptual and instrumental tools the paradigm supplies [Kuhn, 1970, p. 37].

Table 6.1 illustrates how metaphorical frames are embedded in Kuhn's language here. I have based Table 6.1 on two metaphorical frames, *science* and *agency*. In each column, I italicize the words that I believe reflect the metaphor, the surrounding language is included for the sake of context.

In Table 6.1, you'll notice that the metaphors implicit in Kuhn's language are not necessarily the literal words he used. Lakoff and Johnson (1980) and Schön (1993), among others, have shown that although the "surface language" of narrative may not be metaphorical, its *frame* can be

**Table 6.1.  Exemplars of Science and Agency Excerpted from Kuhn's
*Structure of Scientific Revolutions***

| Science | Agency |
|---|---|
| A *scientific community* acquires with a *paradigm* . . . a criterion *for choosing problems* . . . | A scientific community *acquires with a paradigm* . . . a criterion for choosing problems . . . |
| *Problems . . . can be assumed to have solutions.* | Only *problems* that the *community will admit* as scientific or *encourage its members to undertake* [are those that are assumed within the paradigm to have solutions]. |
| *Other problems* . . . are rejected as *metaphysical, as the concern of another discipline,* or sometimes as just *too problematic to be worth the time.* | *Other problems* . . . *are rejected* as metaphysical, as the concern of another discipline, or sometimes as just too problematic to be worth the time. |
| [Scientific problems] are . . . *reducible* to the *puzzle form.* | A *paradigm can* . . . *insulate the community* from those socially important problems. |
| [Scientific problems can] be *stated in terms of conceptual and instrumental tools* the paradigm supplies. | They cannot be stated in terms of conceptual and instrumental *tools the paradigm supplies.* |

metaphorical in nature. With that said, take a look at the exemplars in the column labeled Science. For science, valuable knowledge is derived from specifying and solving problems. This is done with *conceptual and instrumental tools*. *Problems undertaken* in science are *assumed to have solutions*; that is, scientists frame problems in ways that they know can be studied empirically. Good knowledge is "warranted knowledge" (Phillips, 1987) that conforms to criteria agreed upon among members of the scientific community. In addition to setting parameters for good problems, the science metaphor makes clear what kinds of problems are not appropriate for empirically driven inquiry—specifically those that are *metaphysical* and those that cannot be answered with the *tools supplied*.

Now look at the Agency column. Members of the scientific community are capable of *choosing* what problems they care to undertake but only within the boundaries of their scientific paradigm. Rather than actively acquiring their paradigm, the language here suggests that a scientific community inherits a paradigm that, in turn, structures how community members think about and practice their work. Paradoxically, Kuhn presents a picture of scientific communities imprisoned, not liberated, by the paradigms that define their practice.

Evaluation is unique. I believe that the eclectic character of our field has freed evaluators to think about issues encountered in practice in ways that more established fields would have dismissed. Yes, our multiple paradigms have proven painful when trying to be precise about what good knowledge is in evaluation. But having to find ways to talk across our differences has made us smarter about how we think about and practice evaluation. By smarter, I mean we have been able to draw on many sources critically and reflectively to frame and reframe dilemmas we encounter in evaluation, to become more sophisticated in our understandings, and to find metaphors that help us act in novel ways. Let me now briefly show how I think this has been the case based on some of the language that evaluators have used to talk about "good knowledge."

Some of our earliest metaphors for how evaluators thought about producing good knowledge came from the social sciences, which, at the time, looked to the natural sciences for models of warranted knowledge (Phillips, 1987). Objectivity and validity guided decisions about how to produce good knowledge. Good knowledge was statistically conclusive, generalizable, and reliable. It was produced by rigorous scientific methods. Problems encountered in practice were addressed with methodological solutions. Greene (1990) presented post-positivism—the paradigm most closely identified with conventional scientific language of good knowledge—as

a method ideology. . . . It proposes ways of testing and revising theories of optimal political-economic-social organization rather than proposing a specific political and economic system. . . . The post-positivist social scientist's job is to participate in the critical community of inquirers whose collective job it is to develop warranted scientific knowledge. . . . Belying its claims for neutrality and consistent with the character of social engineering, post-positivism clearly rests on a value foundation of utilitarianism, efficiency, and instrumentality [pp. 232–233].

In the same paper, Greene characterized two additional paradigms for evaluation practice. Some of the language she used to describe constructivism included "storytelling," "patterns"—in contrast with Kuhn's (1970) "puzzles"—"conflictual," "multiple," and "situated." To describe knowledge in critical theory, she included "practical action," "contradictions," "enlightens," and "catalyzes" (Greene, 1990, pp. 233–243). In carefully selecting the language she uses, Greene highlights significant differences in what counts as "good knowledge" in these paradigms.

As illustrated in this example, our language of evaluation has adapted the scientific metaphor and adopted others as we have developed evaluation into a field in its own right. Framing how we think about evaluation today, Greene (1990) wrote, "The superordinate principles for thinking about evaluation are no longer our cherished methodologies nor even our self-critical questions about our role in the world, but rather the socio-political issues of evaluation audience and interests" (p. 28). This refocusing has stimulated new ways of framing the problem of "good knowledge" and how to produce it. Good knowledge is now tied up with the principles of audience and interest. Our language and the metaphors we use to talk about good knowledge reflect these principles as well.

Preoccupation with issues of audience and interest are evident in metaphors structuring our language of valuing (for example, House, 1993; Schwandt, 1997) and evaluation use (for example, Shulha and Cousins, 1997; Weiss, 1998). As a field, we agree that values are an inevitable part of evaluation. What we disagree about is how to deal with them.

One way that we have talked about values is in terms of "stakeholders." In his book *Professional Evaluation*, House (1993, pp. 117–121) situates "stakeholder" in a larger historical context in the United States. He presents a model of stakeholder-based evaluation that emerged in the context of social unrest and increased awareness of economic inequities. "Unlike the previous utilitarian, technocratic conception, this model of pluralist democracy recognizes the different interests of diverse groups, accounts for social conflict and the lack of social harmony. . ." (House, 1993, p. 118). It bears mentioning that House described stakeholder-based evaluation in a chapter entitled, "Social Justice," and that he called this particular section, "Stakeholders and the Fractured Consensus."

For the moment, let me just raise the possibility that the term "stakeholder" may limit our capacities to imagine new ways of dealing with differences that we encounter in our evaluation practice. Looking beyond the literal, what metaphors do you think are implicated in the language of "stakeholder interest"? How do these metaphors frame how we think about and produce good knowledge? I return to the question of stakeholder interest at the end of this chapter.

In this chapter I've illustrated some ways that our language of metaphors has changed as the domain of what counts as good knowledge has expanded. Our words are not only different; the ways that we frame questions about knowledge and its worth have moved beyond narrowly defined methodological considerations to incorporate the social, political, and moral implications of our evaluation choices. In short, what we have is a significant conceptual shift, not merely a semantic one.

## Using Metaphors in Evaluation Practice

Examining metaphors in language, particularly metaphorical frames, is useful for the field of evaluation as well as in the field when doing evaluation. Inasmuch as evaluators can sensitize themselves to the assumptions and values guiding their practice, so too can we encourage stakeholders to critically reflect on the metaphorical frames in their talk. To illustrate, let me present a few examples from my own work based on a case of community building in higher education.

**Setting the Context.** As noted, to understand the meaning and significance metaphors hold for people, one must examine the context in which they are used. Three contextual factors important to the examples presented next are the program in which community building was to occur, how the cohort of interest came to be, and the purpose of the study itself.

**The Program.** The study's focus was a cohort of thirteen diverse doctoral students in a program of transformative learning at a small alternative graduate school. The program was structured to accommodate nontraditional students and included a two-year residential with a six-day retreat each August followed by three-day intensive weekends September through June. The curriculum was "emergent." That is, within broad guidelines (e.g., foundations), students as a cohort determined the specific content of their studies (e.g., theories of oppression). Together, the program's structure, curriculum, and pedagogical philosophy of experiential learning and collaboration required active participation in one's community. Consequently, much of the students' work together focused on building a learning community that would serve as the testing-ground for the theories of transformation studied and that would afford them practice at being transformative leaders.

**The _Creation Story_.** The cohort that the study focused on was a result of "two births." The first birth was the August 1993 six-day residential retreat where cohort members came together for the first time for their orientation and initial envisioning of their community. At the time the group consisted of nine students (four Euro-American women, four Euro-American men, and one African-American man). The two faculty members were both Euro-American women.

Midway through the retreat, concerns about the composition of the group were raised. Individuals asked: How can you do transformative learning applicable to the real world if our world here does not mirror the composition of the communities surrounding us? How will we challenge our worldviews and integrate multiple ways of knowing in this basically homogeneous group?

After much debate and discussion, the group petitioned the school to reopen admissions and to offer scholarships to students of color. When the group reconvened the following month for its three-day intensive retreat, it had almost doubled in size to include an additional eight students, all of whom were students of color.

The Multicultural Inquiry eXchange (MIX)—this was the name they chose for themselves.

**The Study.** Serving as the empirical portion of my dissertation, the study from which the examples below are drawn from had two primary aims: to examine how the concepts of voice, action, and empowerment emphasized in the literature on collaborative and participatory inquiry played out in a context where both "difference" and "collaboration" were central ideological precepts; and to contribute to the participants' "learning from reflection." While not an evaluative study in the sense that it was contracted for the primary purpose of determining value, the study did assist key stakeholders—in this case the students and faculty—in determining the worth of their community building experiences.

I arrived on site at the beginning of the MIX's second year. At that point it had stabilized to thirteen members: Two African-American women, two African-American men, one Chicano, one Chicana, one Chinese-American woman, two Euro-American men, and four Euro-American women. One faculty member left to join another cohort. I spent approximately ten months studying and occasionally working with the MIX.

For the better part of the year I tried to understand the discrepancies I encountered in the MIX. What had created the gulf between the language of empowerment and inclusion people used and the community building practices within the group? The MIX's Creation Story and what it symbolized to the group (a visible and loud commitment to learning in a diverse community) contrasted sharply with the tensions, disillusionment, and sometimes outright rebellion that I witnessed.

Where were the "inclusion of all voices" in decision making, "experimenting" with multiple forms and structures of learning, creating and maintaining a "nurturing community," "bringing to center stage the many worldviews and ways of knowing" existent within the group, and overturning relations and structures of "oppression" that group members talked about? This is not what I saw happening, at least not most of the time. Instead, I saw time spent negotiating differences when no time to negotiate existed, individuals fighting against each other to be heard in the limited time available, extreme tensions between task and process, and a constant struggle to create conditions that would nurture the development of all members (and not just a few).Metaphors in the MIX's talk—as individuals and as a group—hepled give shape to some of these disparities.

**Metaphors of Collaboration.** One set of metaphors particularly useful to making sense of the community building dynamics in the MIX related to collaboration. In a critical thinking exercise facilitated by an adjunct faculty member, MIXers had the opportunity to reflect on what individuals meant when they talked about "collaboration." Over the course of the discussion, students distinguished between Collaboration with a big "C" and collaboration with a small "c." Underlying collaboration was the metaphor of "Strategy for Work"; Collaboration, on the other hand, was structured around the metaphor, "Philosophy for Life." As Strategies for Work, collaboration was a functional activity employed to get the task at hand done in the most efficacious manner. As a Philosophy for Life, however, collaboration transcended its task-oriented border, becoming a way of being and acting in the world.

The significance of these two metaphors for collaboration was not to be underestimated because the metaphors suggested two very different ideas about how one should participate in his/her community. There were those students to whom participation in the program was about *being transformed* and that meant collaborating with other MIXers to build a community that would support life-changing experiences. For other MIXers, participation *meant learning about (not necessarily experiencing) transformative* learning. These students sought a community that would further intellectual development, one that used collaboration strategically and as necessary.

**Metaphors of Community Building.** As part of my analysis of the MIX's community building endeavors, I examined five metaphors of community building—Art, Battle, Garden, Experiment, and Journey—in use (mostly unconsciously) within the group. While I have discussed these metaphors in depth in another chapter (see Kaminsky, 1999), let me briefly present two that dovetail with the group's metaphors of collaboration.

The Art metaphor highlighted individual-group tensions within the MIX. The form that these tensions took within this metaphor was between "disciplined practice" and "freedom of improvisation." For some MIXers, especially those embracing the idea of Collaboration as a philosophy for life, intuition and improvisation were seen as essential means by which community formed. As one student wrote when reflecting on her own experience, "I now see that if I permitted my psychic stuff to emerge and take shape before imposing structure and sense, I can make sense on a deeper level. To impose logic and expectation on a creative process is to limit and suppress." In contrast, students who tended toward the collaboration as strategy for work model emphasized the importance of structured practice. One of the artists in the group described his perspective this way, "Before dancers or musicians improvise in such a way that is worth doing in front of anybody, they spend enormous amounts of time practicing in structured environments."

Tensions between improvisation and discipline surfaced and resurfaced over the course of the ten months I spent with the group. "Breaking the schedule" and "trusting the process"—phrases used throughout the ten months I spent with the group—represented values that students held about learning in their program and belied deep assumptions about the way to go about doing it. For some, a loose process, one highly responsive to the moment, was the most appropriate to their community partially because it attended closely to the needs of individuals. Others maintained that while "trusting the process" was valuable, discipline to stick with the schedule established by the group was important.

The garden metaphor shed light on other features of the MIX's community building process, drawing attention to the environment in which the group operated. Recall that the structure of the MIX's program included an emergent curriculum that required group members to come to consensus about the specific learning content of their studies. Also recall that the MIX was a product of "two births." Students recruited after the School had been petitioned to reopen admissions were brought into the program with the understanding that issues of race and diversity would constitute some portion of their studies. Many of the original members had not joined the program with that focus in mind, nor had the program materials suggested it. Hence, it seemed that in the differential recruiting for the same but different program, a gap of intentions formed with some standing on the individual focus side, others on the social change side, and still others trying to straddle both of them.

The garden metaphor helped to make sense of how the program's structure and the group's composition interacted to create inadequate conditions for all individuals to burgeon. For some, the interpersonal processing and attention to individual needs created conditions for transformation. The emergent curriculum, in the minds of these people, should contain nutrients that would lead to this end. For others more interested in theory than experiential learning, more interested in social transformation than personal epiphanies, the MIX's soil required a good healthy dose of theoretical and critical fertilizer. What's more, any good botanist will tell you that gardens are set up strategically—some plants grow well in the shadow of others and other plants will overtake a garden if not kept contained (kudzu, mint, and blackberries as just some examples). In short, the garden metaphor suggested that given the surrounding conditions, perhaps the MIX had too much diversity.

## Using Metaphors: Implications for Evaluators

In this chapter, I contend that language, including our language of evaluation as individuals and as a field, is metaphorical. Even our so-called literal language (stakeholder interest, instrumental use, enlightenment, even "good" knowledge) makes use of implicit metaphorical frames. These frames, in turn, structure how individuals make sense of issues facing them, setting both a problem and its (obvious) solution.

In structuring problems, metaphors work to highlight some features and obscure others. In our own evaluation field, the metaphors of good knowledge have highlighted methods, politics, and morality—but rarely do evaluation approaches emphasize all of these aspects simultaneously. In the MIX the art metaphor drew attention to individual-group tensions while the garden metaphor brought into focus the importance of context. What one metaphor obscures, another can reveal.

Metaphors are used consciously and in-use unconsciously. Evaluator know the importance of examining metaphors stakeholders use to describe their experiences. I wonder, though, how often evaluators explore the metaphors in-use unconsciously. These metaphors tend to be deeply embedded into the structure of language and are not always immediately obvious in the actual words people use. As we deconstruct qualitative data and reconfigure it (the sin qua non of most approaches to qualitative data analysis), do we inadvertently dismantle significant metaphorical frames—frames that I've argued powerfully influence how we perceive and later act on problems? What's gained from examining these in-use metaphors? I've suggested two benefits: stimulating critical reflection and thinking about problems in new ways.

Metaphors are powerful. But making use of them has its own set of challenges. Although MIXers and I spent a day critically reflecting on their metaphors of community building, I believe that it happened too late in the group's process to have sustainable impact on how individuals approached their community building activities. Time and timing are important.

Metaphors also can raise as many questions as they do answers. Metaphors are flexible. That's why I think they're powerful. Others less comfortable with ambiguity may find metaphors troublesome to say the least. All that said, I believe that metaphor is a provocative concept for evaluation. To conclude, let me return to the "stakeholder" question that I introduced earlier. Are there frames other than "interests," "stakes," "competing values"? My sense is, yes, we could find better metaphors in this case. Perhaps something that gives form to a more healthy kind of pluralism—not harmonious necessarily but not "fractured" (House, 1993) either.

## References

Black, M. "More About Metaphor." In A. Ortony (ed.), *Metaphor and Thought*. (2nd ed.) New York: Cambridge University Press, 1993.

Cook, T. D. "Lessons Learned in Evaluation over the Past 25 Years." In E. Chelimsky and W. R. Shadish (eds.), *Evaluation for the 21st Century: A Handbook*. Thousand Oaks, Calif.: Sage, 1997.

Greene, J. C. "Three Views on the Nature and Role of Knowledge in Social Science." In E. G. Guba (ed.), *Paradigm Dialog*. Thousand Oaks, Calif.: Sage, 1990.

House, E. R. "How We Think About Evaluation." In E. R. House (ed.), *New Directions in Educational Evaluation*. Philadelphia: Falmer Press, 1986.

House, E. R. *Professional Evaluation: Social and Political Consequences.* Thousand Oaks, Calif.: Sage, 1993.

Kaminsky, A. "Myth, Meaning, Multiplicity, and Metaphor." In T. A. Abma (ed.), *Telling Tales: On Evaluation and Narrative.* Advances in Program Evaluation, no. 6. Stamford, Conn.: JAI Press, 1999.

Kuhn, T. S. *Structure of Scientific Revolutions.* (2nd ed.) Chicago: University of Chicago Press, 1970.

Lakoff, G., and Johnson, M. *Metaphors We Live By.* Chicago: University of Chicago Press, 1980.

Mertens, D. M. "Inclusive Evaluation: Implications of Transformative Theory for Evaluation." *American Journal of Evaluation,* 1999, *20* (1), 1–14.

Phillips, D. C. "Validity in Qualitative Research: Why the Worry About Warrant Will Not Wane." *Education and Urban Society,* 1987, *20* (1), 9–24.

Schön, D. A. "Generative Metaphor: A Perspective on Problem-Setting in Social Policy." In A. Ortony (ed.), *Metaphor and Thought.* (2nd ed.) New York: Cambridge University Press, 1993.

Schwandt, T. A. "The Landscape of Values in Evaluation: Charted Terrain and Unexplored Territory." In D. J. Rog (ed.), *Progress and Future Directions in Evaluation: Perspectives on Theory, Practice, and Methods.* New Directions for Evaluation, no. 76. San Francisco: Jossey-Bass, 1997.

Shadish, W. R., Cook, T. D., and Leviton, L. C. *Foundations of Program Evaluation: Theories of Practice.* Thousand Oaks, Calif.: Sage, 1991.

Shulha, L. M., and Cousins, J. B. "Evaluation Use: Theory, Research, and Practice Since 1986." *Evaluation Practice,* 1997, *18* (3), 195–208.

Weiss, C. "Have We Learned Anything New About the Use of Evaluation?" *American Journal of Evaluation,* 1998, *19* (1), 21–34.

Whitmore, E. (ed.). *Understanding and Practicing Participatory Evaluation.* New Directions for Evaluation, no. 80. San Francisco: Jossey-Bass, 1999.

ALEXIS KAMINSKY *is an acting assistant professor of education at Stanford University.*

7

*If the purpose of evaluation is learning, dialogue can be
an effective means for achieving this purpose. This chapter focuses on the crucial role of language in establishing
the heuristic stance that fosters dialogic inquiry and
thereby enhances the effectiveness of evaluation. The role
of the evaluator in facilitating dialogue is explicated
through examples from practice.*

# Dialogue for Learning: Evaluator as Critical Friend

*Sharon F. Rallis, Gretchen B. Rossman*

Traditionally, evaluation has served as a technical task by instrumentally
informing decisions at the program or organization level, adding to accu-
mulated understandings of policymakers, and legitimizing politically driven actions (Weiss, 1998). In this chapter, we argue that, in the twenty-first
century, one genre of evaluation can take on a different and greater role
through a commitment to social justice and that the fundamental purpose
of evaluation in this genre is learning. Learning in a postmodern era requires
dialogue; language can either enable or discourage dialogue. This chapter
contributes to an alternative view of evaluation as learning for social justice.
We illustrate the use of dialogue and the power of language in learning
through examples drawn from practice.

In this genre, evaluation aims to serve the deep ethical purposes of a
social program or an organization to influence the fair and equitable distribution of social goods and to foster a more civil society. In a 1991 review of
evaluation and social justice, Ernie House wrote:

> During the past twenty-five years of institutionalized evaluation, we have
> moved from a conception of justice in which it was assumed that increasing
> the economic production of the nation and the outcome measures of a pro-
> gram would benefit everyone alike to a conception of justice in which we see
> that social programs may have different effects for different people and groups.
> During this time injustices regarding race, gender, and ethnicity have been rec-
> ognized by evaluators though not always remedied. . . . [S]hould evaluators
> represent within their evaluations the interests and needs of those unjustly
> ignored . . . and give weight to those interests? I believe [that] position is

morally correct and will be seen so historically. Evaluators cannot be value neutral in these matters. Our conceptions and even our methodologies are value laden [House, 1991, p. 245].

Evaluators in the postmodern world accept that values are present in evaluation. In reminding us that evaluation is not merely a determination of goal attainment, Scriven (1993) argues that absolute values (those that transcend practical concerns) operate in any ethical evaluation, and that "it is truly unethical to leave ethics out of program evaluation" (p. 30). Greene argues that "advocacy" or an explicit value commitment, is an "inevitable part of evaluative inquiry" (1997, p. 26) because claims to knowledge are grounded in the inquirer's own perceptual frame which is comprised of his or her unique experiences, interests, theoretical understandings, value, and beliefs.

The gods of objectivity and impartiality are challenged by a more democratic pluralism. Evaluation approaches or methodologies have adapted to include multiple perspectives and to articulate operating assumptions and ideals (Patton, 1997). As Greene says, the borders between the act of evaluation and the program being evaluated should be opened up:

In this way, evaluation and program can work in concert to help democratize the conversation about equitable health care for the elderly, about generational and spatial destitution, about kids killing kids, about a safe and adequate food supply [Greene, 1997, p. 29].

The democratic pluralist approaches are not relativistic; they are realistic. Rather than represent only the voices of power, they include the voices of those affected or of those likely to be affected by the program. They not only recognize the political dimension of evaluation; they interact with the body politic. They are democratic in essence and more participatory and collaborative than traditional approaches to evaluation.

Given these arguments about evaluation and its development in the recent past, we suggest that the fundamental purpose of evaluation can be *learning*. Where that is the purpose, a thoughtful, ethically conducted evaluation generates information that may lead to shifts in understanding of various stakeholders. These new understandings can be used to improve, strengthen, and/or alter aspects of the program. Stakeholders might be funding agencies, government agencies (at several levels), clients and potential clients of the program, as well as those who administer and implement the program. Learning should be evident at multiple layers in the program and among key stakeholder groups. This focus on *evaluation as learning* represents one conception of evaluation and its use, consistent with the ideas discussed above. This conception shifts our attention to what happens during the evaluative process and at its conclusion and offers new roles for the evaluator.

If learning within and next to the program is the ultimate goal of evaluation, dialogue is essential. Bohm (1990) differentiates dialogue from discussion. The root of discussion is *discutere* with a primary meaning of "dash to pieces, disperse, drive away, dispel, shake off, set free" and a secondary meaning of "examine by argument, debate, talk about *with* another person" (Brown, 1993, p. 689, emphasis in original). The primary meaning evokes the notions of percussion and concussion, suggesting striking or hitting with a connotation of finality. Dialogue, on the other hand, comes from the Greek *dialogos* meaning "conversation, discourse, valuable or constructive communication" (Brown, 1993, p. 661). Dialogue, therefore, is a fundamentally interactive process of authentic thinking together. It is generative. It moves beyond any single individual's understanding to produce new knowledge (Senge, 1990). And it entails a sustained democratic relationship between people—program people and the evaluator.

Why is this relationship so important? In an ideal world, individuals would be reflective and critical of their work, and programs would engage in self-sustaining and developmental learning—they would be *inquiry-minded organizations* (Rallis and MacMullan, forthcoming). Through ongoing monitoring and assessment, conscious and intentional (mindful) reflection, and internal dialogue, the program or organization would identify strengths and weaknesses. As a whole, it would implement appropriate mid-course corrections to address areas of weakness and would be continually on the lookout for blind spots and emergent problems. In this ideal world, external evaluators would not be needed because the culture of the program or organization would demand that all personnel engage in evaluating their goals and activities as a matter of course. Such programs are evaluation-minded.

The full-time inquiry-minded program, however, is rare, and people—not organizations—use evaluation information (Patton, 1997, p. 43). Neither time nor structures exist for dealing with an entire organization, nor can there be assurance that such large-scale interaction or commitment is possible. People—not organizations—turn data into information for its use as knowledge. It is the personal relationship between people that facilitates information use for learning. Through dialogic inquiry, the evaluators help generate the data and encourage the interpretations that foster learning. They help surface troubling questions, hidden data, alternative explanations. They can help program personnel see that the emperor may in fact have no clothes on.

To be heard, however, the evaluator must be more than noise in the system. Rather, she is someone the emperor knows and can listen to. She is more friend than judge, although she is not afraid to offer judgments. She does not fit the traditional image of the evaluator as one who determines the fate of a program. Instead, she is integral to program development. She helps the program people uncover and articulate the program's theories of practice (Argyris and Schön, 1978) and to consider the efficacy of those theories.

At the same time, the emperor has to be willing to attend and listen. If key program individuals are not open to making their assumptions explicit, to examining the data thoughtfully and with open minds, to critiquing existing patterns and interpretations, to considering alternative perspectives, to exploring and proposing new practices, the relationship will go nowhere. The evaluation will not be used. In the relationship fostered by a conception of evaluation as learning, however, program people are able to listen. The evaluator and the program people become *critical friends*.

## Evaluation as Dialogic Inquiry

Partners in the critical friends relationship share a mind-set and commitment that differentiate them from traditional evaluators and enable them to engage in productive dialogue. Their stance is heuristic and critical; their interactions are reciprocal; their shared commitment is toward a more ethical world based on principles of social justice. These stances establish the preconditions for dialogic inquiry.

First, the critical friends take a *heuristic stance*—one that is open to discovery. They realize that knowledge is iterative; it builds on itself. One discovery leads to further discoveries. They seek meaning more than a single truth. Dialogic inquiry is grounded in the epistemologic assumption that truth—or knowledge—is not a given; it is constructed through the learning of individuals and groups. It therefore requires that participants be open to the discovery of multiple meanings.

Heuristic, from the Greek for *discover,* also implies personal insight and tacit knowing (Polanyi, 1966). Tacit knowing, or intuition, is deep inner understanding; it is unarticulated knowledge that derives from experience. Out of this knowing come the hunches that often drive evaluative questions and insights. The critical friends accept the value of tacit knowing; their goal is its articulation.

Critical friends also take a *critical stance,* one that is willing to question the status quo and demand data to guide ethical decisions about change. The word *critic,* from the Latin for one who is decisive and the Greek for one who is able to discern or to separate, implies an individual who can separate out and judge the merits and faults of an object, activity, event, work, or person. The critical stance seeks both positive and negative feedback for the purpose of improving the whole. The term *critical* also means materials and conditions that are essential to a project or person at a given point. Thus, from a critical stance, the evaluator and program people raise questions that are essential, that explore the heart of the issue, and that recognize the tentative and speculative nature of any answers.

The critical stance also means that those in the relationship are willing to explore alternative perspectives. The critical stance of the partners allows their choices for action to emerge from collaboratively discovered meanings, rather than from a separately defined and external truth. Critical questions are grounded in a social justice framework and seek to discover a more just way of being. A typical social justice questions asks: Whose interests are or are not being served by this program? From the critical stance, the evaluator and program people listen for voices that have been marginalized and silenced. They welcome and use contradictions and diverse viewpoints.

A critical stance also means transition and action. Just as one discovery yields to another, new perspectives demand new actions. As in chemistry, math, or physics, a critical mass or point is that condition or place at which an abrupt change occurs; in developmental psychology, Piaget's notion of organic process identifies a disequilibrium phase that tips the balance from one stage of development to the next. Similarly, a critical stance encourages the reorganization of categories and working theories and, thus, the emergence of new meanings. The partners move through a dialectic process from one equilibrium through critical mass and disequilibrium to a new, more stable state. Their critical stance supports and encourages change.

Moreover, the relationship is *equitable and reciprocal.* It is equitable in that the traditional power relationship between evaluator and evaluand are consciously and deliberately blurred. All parties assume responsibility for the agenda, decisions, and actions. Critical friends recognize and value the unique contributions of the other and understand that true dialogue entails give and take. They come together for a common purpose, and they develop shared meanings about where the program is, the value of its status, and where it should go. They determine actions according to their new understandings.

Several contextual conditions encourage dialogue. One crucial ingredient is *mutual ownership* of the process and results. The extent to which program people and key stakeholders are involved in and committed to the evaluation will foster use of the results—their own learning. A second condition is that the *program values* permeate the evaluation. As an example, a participatory literacy project would be ill served by an evaluation that did not track the personal and programmatic changes resulting from engagement in a participatory process. A third condition is that the program people and the evaluator are *mutually respectful*—understanding the complexities of each other's roles and viewing each other as colleagues (Senge, 1990). A fourth condition is that those engaged in the dialogue are willing to *suspend their assumptions* (Senge, 1990; Bohm, 1990). This means that they are willing to surface extant, often-hidden assumptions, articulate them, and examine them for their verisimilitude and coherence. Finally, the evaluator should be *committed* to the broad goals of the program and to seek its greater effectiveness in achieving those goals.

## The Power of Language

Ownership, sensitivity to program values, respectfulness, willingness to examine assumptions, and commitment to program goals are not mere abstractions. Each is enacted in myriad ways as the evaluator and program people and other stakeholders come together and negotiate the meaning of their mutual activity. We argue that it is the language used in and about the evaluation process that enables dialogue. First, without language there is no dialogue. Second, language distinguishes between discussion and dialogue. For example, discussion relies on a language of authority; its finality cuts off the possibility of the interaction that is dialogue. Dialogue, rather, relies on facilitative language, what we have come to call the language of the critical friend. Thus, the language used in these encounters powerfully shapes perceptions and opens up the possibility of learning.

Recent research on learning (Caine and Caine, 1997) asserts that the mind "learns optimally—it makes maximum connections—when appropriately challenged in an environment which encourages taking risks" (p. 107). Commitment, trust, and concern about deeper values help create environments that are safe, ones in which people can be open to new ideas or different perspectives. Such an environment encourages the examination of hidden assumptions and deep values. Alternatively, the mind "downshifts" when it perceives threat (Caine and Caine, 1994, 1997). Perceived threats come in many guises: fear of undue criticism, fear of the unknown, fear of misinterpretation, among others. Thus, to foster evaluation use—learning— the evaluator must focus on involvement and trust, creating learning environments that are challenging without being overwhelming. By the same token, the evaluator must actively avoid creating situations in which program people feel threatened. When they do, their minds shut down and learning cannot occur. We argue that the traditional *language of authority* used by many evaluators and expressed directly in written reports can contribute to defensiveness on the part of potential users and to their shutting down their minds, deflecting the "findings," and . . . filing the report away. When one examines these texts, the language is distanced and distancing, disembodied, and authoritative. The voice of the evaluator in these texts claims to know more about program functioning and results than those involved in the program. In contrast, the *language of the critical friend* is expressed more frequently in dialogue with program participants and key stakeholders. It is thus communicative, personalized, and grounded in program values and ideology. When written, this language communicates shared knowledge.

What does the language of the critical friend do? It enacts dialogue. The dialogue allows mutual identification of what is important—agreement on what is the problem. For example, rather than an authoritative statement, "The program identifies too many students," the critical friend might say, "How are we meeting all of our children's needs?" Dialogue also encourages corroboration and elaboration (Rossman and Wilson, 1994) of explicit insights as well as festering worries. Dialogue can confirm hunches and probe for more detail, pursuing the line of inquiry that "there's more going on here." Next, dialogue can gauge expectations, ensuring that program personnel are realistic about what they expect to accomplish. Finally, dialogue leads to new areas for inquiry. It supports inspiration, initiation, and reconceptualization (Rossman and Wilson, 1994), resulting in a more complex picture.

In the following sections, we depict the language of authority and the language of the critical friend. The language of authority is presented in traditional format—a written report—followed by our analysis and commentary. The language of the critical friend is presented through a specific literary device—the dialogue surrounding the evaluation is set in columns. In the left-hand column is dialogue between the evaluator and key stakeholders (in italics); in the right-hand column is our explanation of that communication. We begin with the language of authority to set the scene for the alternative, dialogic language of the critical friend. For both examples, we draw on an evaluation that we conducted of an inclusion effort in a large city school system. The evaluation design included week-long observations in each of ten schools, interviews with principals and selected teachers, a survey of regular and special education teachers, review of relevant documents, as well as lengthy conversations with key stakeholders. We specifically chose this example because it is not extremely authoritative but still subject to the critical friend critique. The reader will note that the language of authority is exclusively text-based—excerpts from an evaluation report—while the language of the critical friend is presented in dialogue form (based on real conversations), drawing on excerpts from the same report. These excerpts are presented orally and in the context of a relationship.

### The Language of Authority

**Evaluation of the New Birmingham Schools Inclusion Initiative, Final Report**
Principal leadership is crucial for the successful practices of inclusion in the eight sample schools. In those schools that exhibit promising inclusionary practices, the principals espoused clear and strong visions and enacted processes to see that these visions were implemented. The principals offered facilitation and support in various forms to faculty and staff in their complex dealings with students. For example, one principal brought in a university partner to lead inclusion teachers in discussions about modifying curriculum. Another principal consolidated his para-professionals for use in inclusive classrooms.

At the same time, many of the organizational structures and policies of the New Birmingham Public Schools appeared driven by bureaucratic considerations rather than educational ones. In every school, structures and processes exist that support or impede inclusion. These include: class size; student placement; staffing patterns; and programmatic options.

First and foremost, successful inclusion requires small classes with 15–18 students, depending on the needs of the students included. Ideally, these classrooms are staffed by two adults, either two certified adults in a co-teaching arrangement or one certified professional with one para-professional. The standard student:teacher ratio of 28 : 1, set by NBPS policy and supported by board budget, forced principals to seek external resources or to creatively allocate existing resources to reduce class size. Even those schools with smaller class sizes built into the model (as at Oliver) appeared to need further adult support. It is unreasonable to expect that one adult alone in a classroom with as many as twenty students can effectively respond to and meet the diverse learning and behavioral needs that are present in an inclusive classroom.

District policies for placing students in classes also appeared counter-productive to inclusion efforts.

While the report is generally helpful and supportive and provides details, it does not reveal that the program people were involved in generating data or that they collaborated in constructing the resulting claims. The tone shows respect on the part of the evaluator/author for the program; we have no direct evidence from the text that program people also respect the views of the evaluator and hence are likely to use this report. The report stands on its own, with no apparent supporting dialogue that would foster creative, thoughtful use. The report identifies strengths and weaknesses in this inclusion initiative, but it does not depict moments of deep insight that could result in new directions for program goals and activities.

Many of these same "findings" are presented in Table 7.1, in the dialogue between the evaluator as critical friend and program personnel—in this case, school principals. The context of the relationship supports the potential for sustained, thoughtful use. The role of the evaluator, moreover, is that of facilitator and constructive critic.

The dialogue is not always comfortable, and the language is not judgment free. In fact, judgments play an important role in understanding the program and in challenging basic assumptions that program staff hold about program theory and operation. Judgments also surface discrepancies between espoused theories and theories in use (Argyris and Schön, 1978). They can pose the larger, often quite difficult, issues raised at the beginning of this chapter about social justice and those marginalized, even excluded, from the dialogue.

Because evaluation may deal with deeply held issues, this dialogic approach is not always possible. For example, we can imagine an evaluator adopting the formal language of the critical friend without the underlying respect for program values and personnel. In such a scenario, the language may become rote and potentially manipulative rather than genuine and facilitative. In another scenario, an evaluation may be mandated; program staff may be highly resistant to change, or deep divisions may exist. In this second situation, the resulting tension may undercut the mutual respect needed for dialogue to occur.

When effectively implemented, however, dialogue introduces an action-research cycle not dissimilar to the Argyris and Schön double-loop learning stages (1978) or stages identified for critical collegiality (Lord, 1994, in Armstrong, 1998). This cycle includes, first, assessment—taking the pulse of the program and its practices; identifying puzzles and surprises, both positive and negative; and clarifying problems related to practices. Second, it

### Table 7.1. The Language of the Critical Friend: *Meeting of New Birmingham Schools Principals with Evaluator*

E: evaluator; P1: principal 1; P2: principal 2; P3: principal 3

E: *I am pleased that you all could meet with me today. You'll recall that the last time we met, we reviewed data on leadership. Based on the interview results, we agreed that not only is this an important area, but it may be one where the New Birmingham Schools excel. But we also agreed that you are having some problems with inclusion efforts. A couple of you felt there are a lot of things you have no control over—no matter how good your leadership skills. So you asked me to look at some organizational factors.*

Here the evaluator names the problem, together with program people. Note the use of *we.*

P1: *My faculty was glad to see you around again. A few even commented that they felt they learned a lot from the focus group you ran.*

The evaluator is responsive to program needs. The principals' "asking" the evaluator to pursue certain lines of inquiry shows ownership on their parts.

E: *Good. I want to thank you again for facilitating my meeting with the school folk. Three of the schools decided that focus groups were the best way to collect useful data. In the others, we set up individual, and in a few cases, team appointments. They all felt I needed to observe classes for myself. But they agreed to collect the achievement data on students.*

Note also the mutual decision making about the role of the evaluator. Also note the involvement of the principals as key data gatherers, indicating their commitment and ownership of both process and results.

P2: *I get the feeling that you surfaced some problems—at least in my school. What are we doing wrong?*

E: *I did hear—and see—some things that I think are barriers to successful inclusion— but I'm not sure you are **doing** something* **wrong.** *Rather, it may be that you cannot do some things* **right** *because of some of the system's structures and policies.*

This language signals respect, avoids assigning blame to program people, and establishes realistic expectations. It asks the principals to suspend their assumptions about their own behaviors.

P1: *What do you mean?*

E: *First and foremost, it is clear from the interviews and observations that, with few exceptions, your staff are committed to meeting the needs of all the children in their classes. Nevertheless, they make it clear that successful inclusion requires small classes—fifteen to eighteen students, depending on the needs of the students included. And, ideally, classrooms need to*

Mutual respect is evident here. The evaluator begins with positive, supportive language.

Here the evaluator offers a tentative insight for corroboration (or not) by the principals.

**Table 7.1. The Language of the Critical Friend:** *Meeting of New Birmingham Schools Principals with Evaluator (cont'd)*

be staffed by two or more adults. Teachers tell me that sometimes two certified professionals coteaching works well; others say there are times when a certified professional only needs a paraprofessional in the room full time. Even in Oliver, which was designed to have small classes, the teacher needs the support of another adult in the classroom. The consensus is that one adult alone in a room with as many as twenty students just can't effectively respond to—and meet—the diverse learning and behavioral needs that are present in a truly inclusive classroom.

The evaluator understands and is committed to the program's underlying values. Teachers are acknowledged here as important sources of data and insight. The program's values of serving all children permeates the evaluator's language. This helps set realistic expectations and implies a suspension of assumptions.

*P3:* No kidding. That's why I spend so much of my time seeking external resources to fund the paras in my school.

The evaluator is not making judgments at this point, but reporting what she has seen and heard.

*P2:* And I've come up with ways to allocate my Title I and bilingual funds to reduce class sizes.

The dialogue continues to define and clarify the problem.

*E:* I know you do—and so do the teachers. They appreciate your efforts—that's more evidence of your leadership skills. Anyway, I've some strong statements from teachers about the need for reduced class size and adult support in inclusive classrooms. Also, the teachers at each school compiled the configurations of size, support, identified needs, and behavioral and learning needs for their classrooms. You can see that students in the smaller classes have more time on task and exhibit fewer disruptions. You might want to look at grades and scores in those classes to see how the kids are learning.

This illustrates mutual respect and further acknowledges the voice of the teachers in the dialogue.

Teachers are directly involved in the evaluation rather than having it "done to them."

Here the dialogue initiates a new idea for consideration.

*P2:* We should look at outcomes, and grades as one indicator of outcomes. We have the scores, and I can compile grades for each class. Right now, we are just assuming that the children in the smaller classes are learning what they should— I'd like some evidence that they are. After all, the whole purpose of inclusion is to improve **all** students' learning.

The principal develops the idea.

Program values are paramount here.

*E:* Now, another concern is student placement. Teachers and staff regaled me with instances of students sent to them because "there is a seat," not because the appropriate program or services are available.

The evaluator corroborates and elaborates on concerns and "worries" of program people, thereby validating their perspectives. There is evidence of deep respect here.

**Table 7.1. The Language of the Critical Friend:** *Meeting of New Birmingham Schools Principals with Evaluator (cont'd)*

| | |
|---|---|
| *Teachers report frustration when they don't feel professionally prepared to meet the severity of a student's needs.* | |
| *P1: We know that happens—because of certain labeling policies. I'm a victim of those policies too. Like when Central Office sent that full "Lab" program to my building in September—no time to prepare.* | Principal corroborates deep learning and assumes responsibility for program limitations . . . |
| *[discussion continues with reference to staffing and programming]* | |
| *P3: I think we have some pretty powerful findings—ones that need to be addressed before inclusion can be completely successful. But any recommendations to follow what we've learned are likely to require more money. Just dropping a report of this information on the superintendent and board risks it being buried or filed with no action.* | . . . and solutions. |
| | Realistic concerns can surface here as problems for the group to solve. |
| *E: This evaluation documents your needs. It is possible the board hasn't ever seen this information. And Dr. Painter may be unwilling to ask the board for money for more staff or paraprofessionals without evidence of substantial needs. Let's talk about how we can use the documentation to bring about some improvement.* | New possibilities for understanding the larger district context are presented for the group to consider. |
| *P2: Let's take the James, my school. You've got the data that demonstrates the difference in math achievement after we lost Title I funds for that remedial math teacher last year. The Board might be persuaded to support her whether we have federal bucks or not!* | Possible actions are identified here. |
| *P3: You only use her half time, don't you? The intermediate grade math scores in my school are pretty low—could we present a case for splitting her between our schools?* | New directions and creative solutions are put forward. |

includes conscious mutual reflection on the program and practices, including data collection, analysis, and interpretation; third, judgment and reframing or reconceptualizing the program or practice; and fourth, taking action—developing and implementing new program directions or new practices. As the examples demonstrate, language helps establish the environment of trust, risk-taking, and respect that are crucial for the deep learning that is the fundamental purpose of this dialogic genre of evaluation.

## References

Argyris, C., and Schön, D. *Organizational Learning: A Theory of Action Perspective.* Reading, Mass.: Addison-Wesley, 1978.

Armstrong, K. "Reflective Practice and Critical Collegiality: The Experience of Eight Urban Teachers." Unpublished doctoral thesis proposal, Howard Graduate School of Education, Harvard University, 1998.

Bohm, D. *On Dialogue.* Ojai, Calif.: David Bohm Seminars, 1990.

Brown, L. (ed.). *The New Shorter Oxford English Dictionary on Historical Principles.* Oxford, United Kingdom: Clarendon Press, 1993.

Caine, R. N., and Caine, G. *Mindshifts: A Brain-Based Process for Restructuring Schools and Renewing Education.* Tucson, Ariz.: Zephyr Press, 1994.

Caine, R. N., and Caine, G. *Education on the Edge of Possibility.* Alexandria, Va.: Association for Supervision and Curriculum Development, 1997.

Greene, J. C. "Evaluation as Advocacy." *Evaluation Practice,* 1997, *18* (1), 25–35.

House, E. "Evaluation and Social Justice: Where Are We?" In M. W. McLaughlin and D. C. Phillips, (eds.), *Evaluation in Education: At Quarter Century. Ninetieth Yearbook of the National Society for the Study of Education, Part II.* Chicago: University of Chicago Press, 1991, pp. 233–247.

Polanyi, M. *The Tacit Dimension.* New York: Doubleday, 1966.

Patton, M. Q. *Utilization-Focused Evaluation: The New Century Text.* (3rd ed.) Thousand Oaks, Calif.: Sage, 1997.

Rallis, S. F., and MacMullan, M. "Inquiry-Minded Schools: Opening Doors for Accountability." *Phi Delta Kappan,* forthcoming.

Rossman, G. B., and Wilson, B. L. "Numbers and Words Revisited: Being 'Shamelessly Eclectic.'" *Quality and Quantity: International Journal of Methodology,* 1994, *28,* 315–327.

Scriven, M. *Hard-Won Lessons in Program Evaluation.* New Directions for Program Evaluation, no. 58. San Francisco: Jossey-Bass, 1993.

Senge, P. *The Fifth Discipline: The Art and Practice of the Learning Organization.* New York: Doubleday Currency, 1990.

Weiss, C. "Have We Learned Anything New About the Use of Evaluation?" *The American Journal of Evaluation,* 1998, *19* (1), 21–34.

SHARON F. RALLIS *is professor of education at the University of Connecticut. She and Gretchen B. Rossman are co-authors of* Dynamic Teachers: Leaders of Change *(Corwin Press, 1995) and* Learning in the Field: An Introduction to Qualitative Research *(Sage, 1998). Their interests are in qualitative evaluation methodology and school-based change.*

GRETCHEN B. ROSSMAN *is professor of education at the University of Massachusetts.*

8

*This chapter ethnographically documents "lessons learned" in an evaluation of a tuberculosis program, focusing on linguistic rich points gathered from interviews and conversations with program staff.*

# Border Lessons: Linguistic "Rich Points" and Evaluative Understanding

*Michael Agar*

In the spring of 1996, I was invited to "evaluate" a tuberculosis (TB) screening program run by Johns Hopkins University medical center in the city of Baltimore. The Baltimore program, like the other four city programs funded by the Robert Woods Johnson Foundation (RWJ), had already shown that, by traditional outcome measures, things hadn't gone so well. The numbers simply weren't adding up to a success story. For that reason, RWJ looked for something different from ethnographic research, namely, something that would show that all the money hadn't been spent for nothing. As the project director emphasized at a meeting, all five city projects aimed to cross "borders," to connect health care institutions with marginalized populations. He asked that the new evaluations deal with the nature of the border at each site. Representatives from the foundation, at that same meeting, asked for lessons learned, for results that would teach the reader about what worked and what didn't, and why.

I'm more experienced with organizational development (OD) models from the private sector (Argyris and Schön, 1996; Schein, 1999; Senge, 1990), than with evaluation models from the social service sector. OD translates easily into what I call the study of *languaculture* (Agar, 1994), namely, a focus on surface forms of language as a means to the end of modeling the presuppositions and implicatures that explain their meanings, meanings that

The assistance of R. Owen Murdoch and the support of Robert Woods Johnson Foundation Grant #26838 are gratefully acknowledged, as is support from National Institutes of Health grant RO1DA10735.

lead the researcher beyond the words into the nature of the speaker's world. So OD is what I offered to do and, a bit wary of it all, the project team accepted the deal.

Languaculture, I should add, is simply a conceptual summary of a premise rooted in the linguistic anthropological traditions of Sapir and Whorf. In contrast with the assumptions of Chomsky and his intellectual descendants, language is viewed as much more than syntax and lexicon. Instead, language is linked seamlessly with background knowledge that is a product of biography, history, and culture. To interpret and use a language, then, this background knowledge is as critical as mastery of the surface linguistic details. Conversely, if one is interested in the background knowledge of persons and communities, those surface linguistic details offer a publicly available place to start the investigation.

In spite of time and resource limits on the evaluation, the OD/languaculture model easily applied. With a languacultural approach, the researcher looks for surprising occurrences in language, problems in understanding that need to be pursued—linguistic "rich points" are what I call them. The first surprise was that the institution was reluctant to talk, at all. Indeed, the Baltimore research began months after the other cities. First encounters with mid-level staff revealed low morale. Mid-staff and community health workers were reluctant to be interviewed. Some of the principals ignored repeated phone and e-mail messages for months.

This negative organizational climate was of course already a bad sign. Such Foucault-like barriers around discourse flag severe problems, a long list of topics that have become taboo to discuss with outsiders. Nonetheless, once interviews began, several specific rich points did surface in the language of interviewees. In this chapter I will focus on two linguistic rich points in particular—the surprising assertion of outreach workers—community health workers—that the program succeeded, and the dissolution of the partnership between Hopkins and a community-based organization. Between those two rich points another will be treated that both entailed—just what exactly is the "community" in "community screening"?

## Why Were the Outreach Workers More Positive About the Program Than Anyone Else?

Given the interest in the border and lessons learned, the community health workers (CHWs) looked like a promising starting point. The CHWs had the most experience mediating between the community and the health care institution; they could teach us which border connections had worked and which had failed from their personal experience.

It surprised me when I first met with a CHW and talked about the program. I was astounded to hear an animated description of activities that, from the CHW's point of view, began with the project and continued into the present. As more CHW conversations and interviews were conducted, the same theme was repeated—they had gone out and figured out how to do their job and were still doing it. Though frustrations were expressed over lack of leadership, by and large CHWs felt that the Baltimore program was alive and well, in contrast with what other staff and foundation representatives had said.

The CHW sense of satisfaction derives from the *caring model,* a term frequently used by CHWs in interviews and conversations. As long as CHWs were helping people with the constellation of problems they faced, and educating them about TB and those other problems, CHWs felt that their work was worthwhile. Their satisfaction did not depend only on whether they delivered new TB cases or saw that a released prisoner completed medication. The principal goal of the Johns Hopkins program was for the CHWs only one among many, and among those many others goals were several that could be and were in fact achieved.

The overriding themes in the CHW interviews feature affective rather than cognitive orientations to contact with clients, holistic rather than problem-specific concerns, and service based on shared knowledge rather than the acquisition of research information. Most used the term *caring* to describe their work; hence the caring model. In fact, the term is a leitmotiv in conversations and interviews. One outreach worker put it this way:

> Well, caring for people, I believe, is the most important part of it. When you're working in the prison, and they can spot a phony person, and if you go in there and you're phony, they'll spot you right offhand. And they know if you care or don't care.

As one more example of the theme, consider this excerpt:

> It's not for them. And how can I tell? I tell because you don't want to do your job. When you're supposed to be there, you're not there. When I need something from you, or when I have told you that such and such inmate is waiting for you to come back, you don't go back. You don't care. That tells me you don't care.

*Caring* is so frequently used, so tied into manifold aspects of how CHWs describe their work, that it warrants more ethnographic investigation.

The caring model allows the CHWs to see an opportunity where other program staff would describe a problem. Project research shows that TB is not a particularly salient issue among the populations that the project tried to reach. Program clients are people who often suffer from multiple life problems, including racism, violence, poverty, dysfunctional families, drug and alcohol abuse, and other health problems. From the health care point of view, this boils down to a problem in conveying the importance of TB. From a CHW caring point of view, it means that one cannot *just* focus on TB:

And having other resources, letting them know that this TB infection is very important, but if they have other priorities first, they're not going to worry about taking medicine. So you should have other resources. Like if they get out, and they don't have no money, or they need somewhere to stay, or they need a referral with social services, you should have all that information. You should have some resources to send them to. A lot of them have children. Get phone numbers and stuff for who they could talk to get their children back, or what can they do.

Another CHW mentioned that in program training they were told to be "resource persons," which she interpreted as this:

So we were able to do things . . . if they didn't want the TB test, but they were able to get this. Now that's not on the survey or the forms that we filled out. Those were just things that—while we were out there it wasn't just about going door to door offering these people five dollars food vouchers or bus tokens or whatever, but it was about really caring for that person, that if, hey, if they didn't want this and they had another concern, that we would be able to do that. And that was not included in the screening, (laugh) so that was just something that we just kind of went out of the way with.

Health "care," as delivered by a modern research hospital like Johns Hopkins, is implemented in a structured institution that regulates access in terms of space and time. The disease dictates the nature and frequency of contact with the person, and those contacts unfold with reference to standardized guidelines imposed from outside the moment. For the CHWs, caring is something that conflicts with this model in several ways. Caring is delivered in noninstitutional, unstructured ways, personally rather than professionally. Matters of time and space are flexible, adaptable to the flow of events in the patient's daily life. Contact with the person may involve the disease—then again it may not. In fact, caring in service of disease X may in fact impact more on problems A, B, and C than they do on X.

The caring model helps understand several other CHW comments. It is no secret that perceptions of Hopkins in East Baltimore are negative, for many reasons, among them the historical use of the neighborhoods as a research laboratory. As one CHW put it:

Right, and Hopkins has a bad name. (laugh) We found that out. That was something else. If we did mention Hopkins, and oh, no. (laugh) There was something to that.

Given this level of frustration with and hostility toward Hopkins, the CHW begins work in the community with a problematic institutional affiliation. As one woman put it at a meeting, "You got people coming out here, our people coming out here asking us these questions. It's not that we don't like our people or that we're against them, but we know who they represent."

Border work is handed off by the institution to black community members, the CHWs. But on the other side of that border, the institution is viewed with skepticism or hostility. Jones, in his chapter on corporate life (1994), mentions how black managers are often charged with what he calls "the relations"—customer relations, community relations, human relations, and the like, often to deal directly with urban black populations in what he calls "velvet ghetto" jobs. In fact, three interviewees, none of them on tape, mentioned that they felt that the expectations were that, since they were black, problems with program implementation were automatically solved. As one CHW said in conversation, "Don't expect me to work magic because I've got a black face."

CHWs represent the institution—Johns Hopkins—and carry the responsibility of making community patients fit institutional designs. On the other hand, CHWs are members of that same community and therefore are expected to speak, understand, and act according to community ways, including community resentment of the institution for which they work. The health care/caring difference represents one shape that the dual affiliation takes. The caring model helps solve the problem, as it shifts the CHW from an institutional identity to a personal, one-on-one encounter.

The concern with caring helps understand other problems mentioned in the interviews as well, "problems" from a CHW perspective that represent normative clinical practice—confidentiality and clinic visit scheduling, for example. Unfortunately, space is not adequate to fully develop them here.

But one other area of project activity proved more difficult for the CHWs—research. A standardized research interview differs wildly from the normal ways a CHW talks in the neighborhoods where outreach takes place. Here the literature on black English becomes relevant, though there are problems in its application that we take up in the conclusion. Smitherman talks about how black communication derives from an oral tradition out of Africa while white communication derives from a print-oriented tradition out of Europe. She cites the psychiatrist Franz Fanon: that to talk like a book is to talk like a white man (1977, p. 77). She also discusses the "linguistic ambivalence" (1977, p. 174) of blacks when they choose between communicative styles, the personal and emotional significance of the code choice. A shift into a white code is historically a signal of leaving the community, of entering into and committing to the white world.

Smitherman also describes the characteristics of black oral tradition, and her description differs from the usual view of how a person should conduct himself or herself in the context of a social research interview. According to the black oral tradition, the following are highly valued: exaggerated language, mimicry, proverbial statements, punning, spontaneity, image making, braggadocio, indirection, and tonal semantics.

Given Smitherman's descriptions, it's no surprise that CHWs criticized the TB program research. Assuming it's fair to say that the prescribed language and interaction style for a standard research interview are about as white as you can get, given what Smitherman suggests, the criticisms make sense. But it's also true that research is even more distant from the caring model than health care is. In research the person is a case or a data point. Research contact with the person must unfold in prescripted ways to maintain scientific control. With research the product is disembodied knowledge, not interpersonal action.

The CHWs mentioned several details. First of all, they were to stand at the door and speak from a standard protocol, while attention was paid by those nearby on the streets. Second, the survey was considered too long. Third, questions involving such areas as income, prison, occasional residence, drug and alcohol use, and sexual practices were seen as too personal and intimate. Fourth, some answers called for time-line estimates that simply did not map onto the way respondents thought about their activities. People were often suspicious—some slammed the door—and they wondered why they had to be interviewed when they had no interest in being tested. And, finally, the neighborhood selected for community screening is a serious crack area. Needless to say, crack houses and crack users are not known for their predisposition to discuss income and hours per day spent at work with CHWs.

Kochman writes that blacks regard as private much of what whites talk about—he quotes a black talking to a white after listening to people on a bus: "Your people don't care who knows their business" (1981, p. 98). And he argues that blacks think the person should control disclosure of personal information; direct questions from another put control in the questioner's hands instead. Kochman claims that requests for information are done by signifying, which he defines as "intending or implying more than one actually says" (p. 99). Direct questions can also be seen as attempts to "front someone off," or get a person to reveal information that would be embarrassing (p. 101).

Kochman also writes that blacks use directness to signify in the sense of implying something negative or accusatory, as in bringing back a diet coke when a person just asks for a coke, or asking about an item of apparel (p. 103). And finally, in a comment that gets directly to the research issue: "Blacks resist information-seeking probes not simply for reasons of etiquette but because, as a minority group, they have been and continue to be vulnerable to the way such information might be interpreted and used" (p. 104).

At this point we should mention that, among the six CHWs we spoke with, all criticized the survey to a greater or lesser extent, but the six varied in their general description of the experience. Two were fairly negative; the others, however, had positive things to say as well. We close with the hypothesis that the problem isn't acquiring and documenting information; rather, it is the scientific requirement for acquiring it in a way that contradicts the caring mode and the communicative norms of situations where interviewing was done.

## The "Community" in "Community Health Worker"

The discussions with, and about, CHWs often led to the topic of whether or not the "right" CHWs were hired for the project, a subject that came up with both mid-staff and the CHWs. Did particular CHWs—as the question often went—really represent "the community"?

The term *community* is used frequently by everyone involved in the Hopkins project. In fact, it is used frequently, period, in contemporary American discourse. One of its uses, in the TB project, described a central part of the intervention, namely, the community screening, the task that was the charge of the CHWs. Now, community carries certain associations. Community connotes a group, families, residence, stability, connection, and shared activities. Is this the kind of "community" in which the TB intervention was conducted?

Conversations and interviews suggested that the "community" had been selected primarily because it surrounded a new health center. It was defined by a census tract rather than any local community name. While the selection appears reasonable given the then-productive collaboration between Hopkins and the community-based organization, called HOPE in this chapter, many interviewees claimed it was not the best area to have picked. Census information on income, crime, housing, education, and health portray an urban area in a state of advanced decay.

But none of this background information prepared me for the impression I received when I first drove to the neighborhood. Since I checked those impressions in several interviews, an excerpt from one of them is presented here (location names changed; M stands for author; I for interviewee):

M: It was weird driving up there, because I hadn't been in that neighborhood before. And you know, I've done a lot of work with drug users over the years, and I pulled up right along Roberts Street, and I'm looking around and I'm thinking, damn, this is serious. I mean, that's a serious crack neighborhood.
I: Yeah, yeah, yeah, yeah. Ronnie had a house over there that was a drug house, before his uncle went over there and busted it up. But we used to just sit in there all day. The other center is here, there's a little street where they've made like a parking lot for the church, right over there, it used to be.
M: Well it just seemed like it was one scene after another up and down the street.
I: That's right.
M: Is that one of the heaviest in the city?
I: Oh yeah, oh yeah, definitely.
M: Because see the reason I was so surprised is I was thinking, community, right. And so I was expecting more—maybe some street action and stuff like that, but also a lot of just folks, you know, working folks. But uh-uh.
I: Roberts Street, MacDonald Street, uh-uh.
M: Heavy scene.

I: Yeah, Orly Avenue. All off that. Cline Street, which is where my mom lives.
M: So that's a hell of a big . . .
I: They should have asked somebody before they just went and set right in the middle of a war zone, you know what I'm saying?

Another CHW pointed out that the census tract did in fact contain working people, older residents, and families, even if it was a heavy drug scene. The previous quote suggests that the tract isn't just a drug scene, either, with comments about a relative in the area. But even the CHW who talked about non-drug-using residents said things like:

I: Oh, it was worse before the Hope Health center, before the center. I mean you could look out the window and see transactions and there's a crack house right across the street. (laugh)
M: That's right.
I: It was bad, because I think they had to delay a lot because people were taking their equipment (laugh) while they were building—
M: While they were building the building?
I: So they finally got it finished.

In what sense is this census tract a community? Even with the qualifications of these two CHWs, one can argue that the community screening was more of a drug-user outreach program. Furthermore, if the census tract is more of a crack neighborhood, then the low rate of response and the low priority on TB that the project documented appear in a different light. Crack users are not known for their general health concerns or their visits to health care centers.

Given that conventional images of community probably had nothing to do with the "community" in which the screening took place, other discussions with project staff also appear in a different light. Earlier in this section, these questions were raised: Were the right CHWs hired? Did the CHWs represent "the community"?

Which community? The down-and-out crack users?

Some interviewees also discussed whether or not the community organization that worked with the project really represented the community. The first level of the question runs like this: A church-based organization with its religious orientation does not represent more secular blacks who view the church with attitudes ranging from indifference to disdain. The second level of the question argues that HOPE is not as well known or as well supported as it thinks it is. The third level, one articulated by a CHW active in a church not affiliated with HOPE, holds that there are churches and there are churches, and those associated with HOPE may stand in a different relationship than others vis-à-vis the community.

HOPE certainly was, and is, an organization with substantial church membership, an organization that implements numerous service programs in several different East Baltimore locations. To argue that it doesn't represent *some* community would be absurd. At the same time, it is reasonable to ask what community it does represent, and whether or not that community included the census tract where the TB screening was carried out.

The problems with the "community" in community health worker leads to the question—of the author of this chapter as well as the TB project: Why didn't the complexities that the community concept conceals become obvious sooner?

One hypothesis is this: border projects are typically established, funded, directed (and evaluated) by predominantly white institutions, and the white model of black America emphasizes homogeneity rather than diversity. Jones, in his work on black managers in business cited earlier, describes how blacks are seen as expert representatives on any and all black issues, as spokespersons for an imagined homogeneous black community. Jones also writes that this—from a black manager's point of view—rather embarrassing problem is difficult to discuss with whites, since whites can't admit to perceptions based on race for reasons ranging from self-esteem to political correctness to possible legal action.

The results, then, look like this from a white point of view: There is a single black community in the United States. Any black person represents it. To probe into the divisions and conflicts and differences that constitute black America, or to question which position a black person holds with reference to those many differences, is to risk making a racist statement.

Though this is a hypothesis, its plausibility is supported by the ambiguities we unearthed; it's not clear what kind of community—we should say communities—the census tract was. Nor is it clear how to sort through the many statements about HOPE or black CHWs and mid-staff to understand which communities a person or organization represents and what it means to do so. Nor is it clear what communities white staff represent. Would a white ex-crack user be a better CHW than a black who viewed drug use as an unspeakable evil?

## Why Did the Hopkins/Community Partnership End?

In this section, we turn to the second major linguistic rich point, this time inspired by the top of the project hierarchy. When the project began, it rested on a successful partnership between a white academic and a black minister, a partnership that had been in place for years prior to the TB program. By the time this research began, the relationship between the white academic and the black minister had ended. The CHWs represent *persons* who cross borders, but the Hopkins/community alliance, embodied in the academic and the minister, represents the *institutional* border crossing that is just as critical.

First, some background: One strong and enduring type of black community organization in both East and West Baltimore is the church. Smitherman, in her book on black communication (1977), describes the centrality of the black church in general. In Baltimore, the churches in the west traditionally had more political power. The Reverend Williams, as we will call him, pastor of a church in East Baltimore, was among a group of ministers who decided that the time had come to put the east side on an equal footing. He helped found a church-based organization that we call HOPE.

Notable in what interviewees told us was HOPE's comprehensive focus around several issues of community concern, ranging from representing East Baltimore in city politics to the many interconnected problems of urban life. This holistic, multilevel orientation is critical to remember in order to understand one hypothesis about the breakdown between the Hopkins TB program and HOPE that comes later. Note that this organizational holism maps neatly onto the holistic nature of the caring model of outreach outlined in a previous section.

About 1990, Professor Jenkins, as we will call her, worked in Urban Health (a pseudonym) at Hopkins. Jenkins learned of the HOPE program and contacted them about collaborating on a smoking cessation project. Together, Jenkins and Williams founded a health-oriented component of HOPE that we call the Hope Health program. The Hope Health program flourished and, to make a very long story superficially short, eventually involved several projects, including a major foundation grant that addressed the border issues that the TB project was concerned with.

An article attests to the success of the collaboration in 1993 in the local daily newspaper:

> A Johns Hopkins researcher and an East Baltimore pastor say that scientists should make community members full partners if they want to encourage blacks and other minorities to participate in health studies. Prof. Jenkins, of the Johns Hopkins Department of Urban Health, and the Rev. Williams, pastor of the Baptist Church, gave the advice during a conference this month at the National Institutes of Health in Bethesda. Conference participants discussed the need to broaden clinical studies, which often have been limited to white men. The session explored ways researchers can recruit women and minorities so that their health conditions will be understood better [*Baltimore Sun*].

And later, in the same article:

> Mr. Williams, who is chairman of Hope Health program, said he was suspicious when Dr. Jenkins approached him. "There was a lack of trust in the workings of the institution. . . . Most of what I knew came from the operation of the emergency room. The service the community received there was sometimes inhumane," he said. . . . Speaking of himself in the third person, he said: "When we started out some 3 $\frac{1}{2}$ years ago, Dr. Jenkins and Reverend Williams were about as far away as Los Angeles and New York. We've got it down to Baltimore and D.C. now." . . . Dr. Jenkins said the community wasn't the only

partner with initial suspicions. Hopkins also had to learn to trust neighbor-hood workers to perform their tasks and administer some of the research grants. "It's a big problem within the institution, trusting the community to be an equal partner" Dr. Jenkins said [*Baltimore Sun*].

To summarize, then, the Hope/Hopkins alliance was a joint effort that anyone concerned with the border would applaud. The history of Hope Health as a site for collaboration between Hopkins and East Baltimore made it the nat-ural place to locate the community-screening portion of the TB program. This history of collaboration, this impressive list of accomplishments, creates an expectation of a smoothly run program with a successful outcome. Yet, as I entered the picture, the collaboration had dissolved. What happened?

The staff of the TB program, in interviews and conversations, offered partial descriptions, usually negative in tone, sometimes laced with personal passions driven by frustration. There was a reluctance to discuss the issue and claims that the speaker didn't know the story. In spite of repeated efforts, attempts to obtain interviews with the academic and the minister did not succeed until the very end of the study. One knowledgeable person spoke with a request for strict confidentiality. And toward the end of the study, a person involved with both HOPE and the university granted an interview.

Accounts of the breakup vary, as might be expected. Jenkins offered a cultural explanation of the breakup. She has been involved in efforts to link Hopkins and East Baltimore for years, including several projects besides Hope Health, and she has taught a course in African-American community culture and health—in coordination with community members—several times. She is amazed, she said, that even after all her years of experience, she still can't fully bridge the differences between Hopkins institutional cul-ture and that of the surrounding community. She thought that HOPE and Hopkins were running on parallel tracks and was surprised at the problems that arose that disrupted the alliance. Her discouraging conclusion is that the country may not be ready for successful black/white partnerships because of the magnitude and subtlety of the differences.

Among the many cultural differences discussed, one will be mentioned here by way of illustration. She contrasted the "fluidity" of black commu-nity life with the "fixed" institutional structures of a place like Hopkins. In community sessions, for instance, leadership is claimed on the basis of the issue at hand rather than on fixed position. Decision making is flexible depending on who is present and their relevant expertise. Funds are viewed as discretionary for whatever program needs arise rather than fixed in cer-tain categories. Note the parallels between fixed and fluid and the contrast between the health care and caring model.

Williams tells a different story. When Hopkins approached HOPE to collaborate on the smoking cessation project, he was by his own descrip-tion a minor figure. But as an East Baltimore person, he knew "the history, the hatred" that the community felt toward the institution. He was assigned to talk to Hopkins for this reason. One quote to explain his decision to form the partnership:

> I became convinced for this reason. I knew that on judgment day if I knew information that could extend the life, the quality of life of people, my people, my parish, then in light of what I was seeing in my community, certainly to change that, and I would have to give an account to God, and it would give me an opportunity to do something that I thought I could do. Little did I know that God had blessed me with the ability to get folks to stop smoking.

Williams, and the minister interviewed later who will be described in a moment, both couch their descriptions and explanations in a religious discourse that is striking when compared with the accounts of all the other professionals.

Williams saw himself as controlling access to community in a time when funding agencies were demanding just that access as a condition of support. His role, he said, was to "keep them honest" by ensuring that resources flowed to community and that services were provided. Control was the issue for Williams. He felt that Jenkins controlled HOPE workers while he was not allowed control over the Hopkins members of the team. He said that Hopkins would shift available monies across funding categories but he was not allowed to do so. He and another minister often voted against Jenkins on the three-person board. He recently learned about indirect costs and wondered why HOPE hadn't received any. In an echo of Jenkins's comments, he said that in spite of how much he appreciated her efforts and the chances she took, she still worked in "the institutional way."

Remarkable in both interviews was the tone of respect and understanding toward the former partner. Both, in fact, said they were writing books about the experience, and it will be a fascinating future exercise to read them side by side. Perhaps a comment by the other minister, the person involved with HOPE but also an employee of Hopkins, is appropriate here: "It's a challenge for two very strong, intelligent people to stay in the kitchen and continuously cook Thanksgiving dinner every day."

It is difficult to untangle personality from identity, but interesting to note that Jenkins attributes the differences to culture while Williams emphasizes that the partnership concept was subverted by dominance of institutional ways. Their contrasting views reflect a long-standing debate over communication problems versus power differential as explanations for conflict. The HOPE/Hopkins story shows that both explanations are relevant. Clearly the difference between institutional and community ways plays a role; clearly, resolution of differences in the direction of the resource-controlling institution was also a major issue.

Two other accounts of the breakup were obtained. The first came from a secular person in a position to observe it. As that person told it, Hope

Health began to take on a life of its own, from the point of view of the ministers who ran HOPE. The same energy that Jenkins put into the founding of Hope Health led to plans for more projects in response to outside interest in the alliance. Positive as this may sound from some points of view, the HOPE ministers apparently started to feel like the tail was wagging the dog, like Hope Health was moving beyond their original concept of local community service and losing its coherence with the many other HOPE activities. Hope Health, in other words, was becoming a Hopkins Institute rather than an arm of HOPE.

The Hopkins TB project, according to this view, simply pulled farther away from the HOPE pattern, in a way that had already become an issue among the HOPE ministers, so that they felt they had to insist on more control. Recall that the Hopkins TB program focused on a specific disease rather than on general community health, and it acknowledged no ties to other issues of concern to HOPE. Second, Hope Health was asked to provide one component of a separate Hopkins project rather than being the organizational and community focus of its own project. And finally, community screening emphasized research as much, if not more than, community service. These characteristics of the Hopkins TB project featured issues that the HOPE ministers were already concerned with before that project started.

The account of this person, then, reflects the mix of culture and control offered separately by the two principals. A second interview, already cited earlier, was conducted with a "bridge" person, a minister involved with HOPE who also works for Hopkins as a community liaison. He also talked of the hostility toward Hopkins, reporting that older members of the community still warn that lone blacks are abducted late at night for medical experiments. For readers who may not know the history, one needs only think back on the Tuskegee experiments on black prisoners, contemporary with those older community members, to understand where the story comes from. He also pointed out that resentment was strong because Hopkins's expansion had displaced community residents. In fact, he credited Jenkins with having accomplished much to improve the image of Hopkins in the community.

Earlier, his comment about the problems of two strong personalities was cited. He also said that, with time, the two of them saw different lines of development for Hope Health, something that the previous interviewee described as well. But he also added that, at base, the two had different "allegiances," Jenkins, an "institutional allegiance," and Williams, a "spiritual allegiance." He felt that if Jenkins had had more of a spiritual background, and if Williams had come to the ministry after years of work at IBM, they might have understood each other better. This issue of religiosity, which threads through both Williams's and the second minister's accounts deserves a study of its own, or so it appears to the secular author of this chapter.

At the end, then, we are left with several explanations of the breakup. First of all, two strong personalities created a dynamic synergy with their initial agreement, but then conflict developed with time as their interests diverged. Second, cultural differences, whether attributed to African-American versus Anglo-American or community versus institution, surfaced in different views of organizational process that caused conflict in communication. Third, institutional control of resources led the community to question the nature of the partnership. And finally, the secular basis of science and medicine and the spiritual basis of the HOPE organization produced conflicting interpretations of program activities.

Before my work began, HOPE employees had moved out of their offices at Hopkins and Hopkins staff no longer worked at the community health center. The outcome is a fact; the explanation of why it occurred is a hypothesis based on what reluctant interviewees were willing to teach me.

## Lessons Learned

There are other stories to tell about the Hopkins program, but the community health workers, the nature of community, and the partnership between institution and community were among the most important. More to the point here, this approach—a mix of languaculture and organizational development—offers a perspective on what *lessons learned* in fact are, given a focus on language and communication.

Linguistic rich points in the language of interviews and conversations with program staff signaled the lessons. Indeed, the study began with rich points, when the program displayed reluctance to have the study done at all. It also ended with linguistic rich points, when local TB program staff—at all levels—found the report illuminating while professional evaluation-trained colleagues judged it to be an unacceptable form of the genre. Unfortunately, limits on this chapter do not allow a full discussion of those issues. However, once interviews began, program-specific linguistic rich points also surfaced, three of which were discussed here.

The first linguistic rich point surfaced when CHWs evaluated the program in a positive light—in contrast with the negative evaluation of virtually everyone else involved. This rich point led to a *concept-based* analysis of interview transcripts around the term *caring*, center of the CHWs positive evaluation of the program. The analysis, in turn, resulted in a model of how the CHWs thought about and conducted their work, a model that differed from the professional models of health care and research in numerous and important ways. Caring versus health care/research, then, defined a lesson about the Hopkins/community border.

The second linguistic rich point, derived from the caring model, zeroed in on the nature of community. Although this, too, was a concept-based analysis, it went beyond the transcripts into several other conversations, observations, and literatures. This second analysis exemplifies the way that languacultural approaches in particular—ethnographic approaches more generally—shift from a specific rich point to a broader exercise in model building (Agar, 1996). *Community* turned out to be a coherent and homogeneous concept on the institutional side of the border, but diverse, even fragmented, in the census tract of East Baltimore. This crucial shift in meaning also defined part of the border.

The third linguistic rich point, the community/institution partnership, shifted from a *concept* focus to a *relational* one, to general communication patterns between human representatives of different institutions. In this case, the rich point was a dramatic one, since communication between those partners had simply disintegrated. The analysis showed how both communication and control differences explained the breakup, how both organizational process and control over resources also defined the border.

Attending to language as a surface representation of what programs are all about certainly proved useful. By focusing on linguistic rich points and the analyses they inspired, much was learned about the program and its historical context in a limited amount of time. And the organizational development framework guided the inquiry rather well. But, in the end, what is this border we've been talking about? The border—supposedly the one between the buildings of Johns Hopkins medical center and the neighborhoods of East Baltimore—is marked by differences of culture, class, and race. It is fair to say that the health care institution is hegemonically upper-middle-class white. The community, around the hospital in East Baltimore, is poor urban black.

So what have we learned here? That the border between Hopkins and community is one of affluent white and impoverished black? We needed a study to figure that out? Certainly interviewees at all levels of the program drew on *white* and *black* to describe and explain part of what they narrated. Indeed, for some a rule almost operated—if a black/white difference is found in the vicinity of a problem, than use that difference to explain that problem. I have done a lot of that in this chapter as well. And perhaps some of the analyses, to echo Jenkins, display the "magnitude and subtlety of the differences." But, in the end, maybe it's not so crystal clear.

First of all, consider the outreach workers. The caring model and the health care model were contrasted in that discussion. To some extent, the different models, with the support of the linguistics literature, were seen as reflecting differences in communication norms between Anglo-American and African-American traditions. But consider that some of the differences between caring and health care are also represented by one of the most robust variables used in intercultural research, the contrast between individualism and collectivism. Or consider the host of analyses of professional and community in numerous applied fields, where the professional has a task-specific, instrumental focus and the community has a more holistic and affective approach. Is caring versus health care just specific to the black/white border? Or is it an example of a much broader problem that calls out for a general model of professional/community interaction?

Now re-examine the conflict between Hopkins and the community program HOPE. Is this problem also only about race? Once again, data does reflect cultural differences, either historical or social-structural, just as in the case of the community health workers. And once again, the alternative explanation of professional versus community orientation to a problem suggests itself. The community/institution breakup also suggests other factors—two strong personalities, changing directions, control over resources and process, and the sacred/secular divide. On the one hand, issues such as the nature of the directions, the distribution of control, and the sacred/secular distinction, can be mapped onto the history of Anglo- and African-American relations in the area. On the other hand, such organizational issues are more universal than a focus on the specifics of the Hopkins TB program would suggest.

Finally, consider the issue of community. Is community in Baltimore just a matter of black and white? First of all, in our postmodern times, groups and identities have lost their edges to the point where such notions as *community* have become controversial in social research, with concomitant problems for sampling and generalization. Second, internal diversity within communities is a political and social issue virtually everywhere in the world. And in social psychology, one robust finding suggests that group members always see themselves as diverse and outside groups as homogeneous. Was the notion of community in the TB program just a matter of race, or was it also a local example of a global phenomenon, where the simple mapping of person onto single community is no longer so easy, neither from the person's, nor from the outsider's, point of view?

Interestingly enough, this ambiguity also blends into the literature on black English as well—or AAVE, African-American Vernacular English, as it has more recently been labeled. The two sources relied on here—Smitherman and Kochman—represent respected but dated work out of the seventies. In both cases the authors say there is no simple mapping from black communication onto any particular African-American person. With the past and present influence of African-American expressions on the linguistic styles of all Americans, we might add that there is no simple mapping of black communication onto anyone. In fact, recent work on the language of African-Americans questions its assumed homogeneity, its distribution, and its similarities and differences with other varieties of American English (Baugh, 1999). Once again, there is something to the notion of a tradition of language and communication that is distinct for African-Americans; on the other hand, persons of African-American and Anglo-American ancestry, at any particular moment, are participating in and drawing from numerous other communicative traditions as well.

As a researcher, and a white, I am now subject to criticism on the basis of the very identity issue I'm addressing. In other words, I can be criticized for defusing the importance of black and white as the major explanatory principle for a border defined in just those terms. Nonetheless, the interviewees—black and white—who taught me about key border issues in the Hopkins TB program also taught me that an a priori commitment to *only* such explanations might miss some interesting possibilities for solutions.

The demographics of race clearly define the context of the program, but the way those demographics played out locally link them to more general issues of organizational process.

I make this argument in the spirit of trying to find a new angle of vision on America's enduring issue of race. Perhaps the tendency to focus on a single program and lump all program difficulties under the powerful and available framework of racial differences is in part responsible for the deadlock so many feel the country is in. That there are problems, and that such problems often fall along a black-white border, no one denies. But based on this brief study, at least some of these problems, lumped together as matters of black and white, could be profitably understood as functions of border issues with other explanations linked to general questions that go well beyond a specific program and the specific issue of race in America. If that is right, such alternative explanations might lead to fresher views and new ideas for solutions. If it's wrong, it would still be worth a try. That's the lesson I learned.

## References

Agar, M. *Language Shock: Understanding the Culture of Conversation*. New York: William Morrow, 1994.

Agar, M. *The Professional Stranger: An Informal Introduction to Ethnography*. (2nd ed.) San Diego: Academic Press, 1996.

Argyris, C., and Schön, D. *Organizational Learning II: Theory, Method and Practice*. Reading, Mass.: Addison-Wesley, 1996.

Baugh, J. *From the Mouth of Slaves*. Austin: University of Texas Press, 1999.

Fanon, F. *Black Skin, White Masks*. New York: Grove Weidenfeld, 1977.

Jones, E. W. "What It's Like to Be a Black Manager." In M. C. Gentile (ed.), *Differences That Work: Organizational Excellence Through Diversity*. Cambridge, Mass.: Harvard Business Review, 1994.

Kochman, T. *Black and White Styles in Conflict*. Chicago: University of Chicago Press, 1981.

Schein, E. H. *The Corporate Culture Survival Guide*. San Francisco: Jossey-Bass, 1999.

Senge, P. *The Fifth Discipline: The Art and Practice of the Learning Organization*. New York: Doubleday Currency, 1990.

Smitherman, G. *Talkin and Testifyin: The Language of Black America*. Detroit: Wayne State University Press, 1977.

*Michael Agar is an independent scholar with Ethknoworks, where he conducts research and consults on projects related to substance use and ethnography and communication. He also regularly runs workshops in organizational and academic settings on qualitative research.*

# INDEX

vs. Girondins values, 50–51; Quebec notions of exclusion/inclusion, 50–51. *See also* Applied linguistics
Lucas, K. J., 29, 34, 42
Luckmann, T., 39

Maccoby, E. E., 60
Madison, A. M., 9, 10, 17, 28
March, J. G., 45, 46
*Meeting of New Birmingham Schools Principals with Evaluator*: language of authority reporting on, 87–88; language of critical friend reporting on, 89t–91t
Memory system, 49–50
Men: body language of, 57–58; findings on conversational styles of, 63–64; floor-taking strategies by, 59–61; leadership emergence by, 61–63; talking time by, 58t–59; topic raising by, 61
Mertens, D. M., 30
Metaphoric language: evaluation perspective of, 71–75; examination of, 11–13; excerpted from *Structure of Scientific Revolutions* (Kuhn), 72t–73; implications for evaluators of, 78–79; used in MIX group study, 75–78; usage and value for evaluators of, 70–71; used in evaluation practice, 75–78. *See also* Evaluation language; Language
*Metaphors We Live By* (Lakoff and Johnson), 70
Midwest Sociological Society (1979 conference), 12
Miller, D., 9
MIX (Multicultural Inquiry eXchange) group study, 75–78
Mixed-sex focus groups: evaluation language in, 56–57; results from cross-case analysis of, 57–64. *See also* Focus groups
MIX's Creation Story, 75–76
Montgomery, J., 12
Morgan, D., 56
Moss, S., 62
Multicultural Inquiry eXchange (MIX) group study, 75–78

National Institute on Drug Abuse (NIDA), 35
Needs assessment, 10

Olsen, J. P., 45, 46
Organizational development (OD) models, 93–94
Oswick, C., 12

Patton, M. Q., 5, 16
Pearce, T., 39
Perceptions: of HIV/AIDS language, 10–11; reconstructed through labeling, 24–26; shaped by language, 14–15; of threats, 86
Peterson, J. A., 29, 42
Philosophy for Life metaphor (MIX group study), 77
Policy communities: evaluation underestimating, 44–45; mobilizing opposing coalitions of, 45–46; Quebec welfare reform, 46–49
Policy language (Quebec welfare reform): described, 46–49; policy learning and, 49–51; as welfare reform tool, 51–53
Policy learning: dynamics of, 49–51; promoted by program evaluation, 43. *See also* Learning
*Professional Evaluation* (House), 74
Program evaluation (Quebec welfare reform): described, 43; policy communities as organized anarchies in, 45–46; policy learning by, 43–45
*The Program Evaluation Standards* (Joint Committee on Standards for Education Evaluation, 1994), 56, 64

Quebec welfare reform: evaluation of, 43–46; improved policy language as tool of, 51–53; inclusion and exclusion concepts of, 50–51; policy language of, 46–49. *See also* Policy language (Quebec welfare reform)
Quimby, E., 34

Racial issues. *See* African-American community
Rallis, S. F., 13, 81
Reconsitution, 49–51
Reeder, H. M., 60
Robert Woods Johnson Foundation (RWJ), 93
Rosenberg, C., 32
Rossman, G. B., 13, 81
Sabatier, R., 33, 43

# Back Issue/Subscription Order Form

Copy or detach and send to:
**Jossey-Bass Inc., Publishers, 350 Sansome Street, San Francisco CA 94104-1342**

Call or fax toll free!
**Phone 888-378-2537 6AM-5PM PST; Fax 800-605-2665**

Back issues:    Please send me the following issues at $23 each.
(Important: please include series initials and issue number, such as EV77.)

1. EV _____

_____

_____

$ _____ Total for single issues

$ _____ Shipping charges (for single issues *only;* subscriptions are exempt from shipping charges): Up to $30, add $5$^{50}$ • $30$^{01}$–$50, add $6$^{50}$ $50$^{01}$–$75, add $7$^{50}$ • $75$^{01}$–$100, add $9 • $100$^{01}$–$150, add $10 Over $150, call for shipping charge.

Subscriptions    Please ❏ start    ❏ renew my subscription to *New Directions for Evaluation* for the year \_\_\_ at the following rate:

❏ Individual $65      ❏ Institutional $118
**NOTE:** Subscriptions are quarterly, and are for the calendar year only. Subscriptions begin with the spring issue of the year indicated above. For shipping outside the U.S., please add $25.

$ _____ Total single issues and subscriptions (CA, IN, NJ, NY and DC residents, add sales tax for single issues. NY and DC residents must include shipping charges when calculating sales tax. NY and Canadian residents only, add sales tax for subscriptions.)

❏ Payment enclosed (U.S. check or money order only.)

❏ VISA, MC, AmEx, Discover Card # _____ Exp. date _____

Signature _____ Day phone _____

❏ Bill me (U.S. institutional orders only. Purchase order required.)

Purchase order # _____

Name _____

Address _____

_____

Phone _____ E-mail _____

For more information about Jossey-Bass Publishers, visit our Web site at:
www.josseybass.com      **PRIORITY CODE = ND1**

OTHER TITLES AVAILABLE IN THE
NEW DIRECTIONS FOR EVALUATION SERIES
*Jennifer C. Greene, Gary T. Henry*, Coeditors-in-Chief